Contents

Introduction	7
1. Leaving to Cleave	9
2. Through Forgiveness to Intimacy	23
3. Sex Role Conflicts	37
4. Prosperity and Adversity	51
5. Cultivating Companionship	63
6. Growing Older Together	77
Notes	91

PRACTICING MARRIAGE

PRACTICING MARRIAGE

Lucy & William Hulme

FORTRESS PRESS   PHILADELPHIA

Excerpt from "Little Gidding" in *Four Quartets* by T. S. Eliot, copyright 1943 by T. S. Eliot, renewed 1971 by Esme Valerie Eliot. Reprinted by permission of Harcourt Brace Jovanovich, Inc., and Faber & Faber, Ltd., London.

Biblical quotations, unless otherwise noted, are from the Revised Standard Version of the Bible, copyright 1946, 1952, © 1971, 1973 by the Division of Christian Education of the National Council of the Churches of Christ in the U.S.A., and are used by permission.

Copyright © 1987 by Fortress Press

All rights reserved. No part of this publication may be reproduced, stored in a retrieval system, or transmitted in any form or by any means, electronic, mechanical, photocopying, recording, or otherwise, without the prior permission of the copyright owner.

Library of Congress Cataloging-in-Publication Data

Hulme, Lucy.
   Practicing marriage.
   1. Marriage—Religious aspects—Christianity.
I. Hulme, William Edward, 1920– . II. Title.
BV835.H85   1987   248.4   86–45916
ISBN 0-8006-1957-9

2656I86   Printed in the United States of America   1-1957

Introduction

Our view of marriage is best described as "Practicing Marriage." We joke about the physician or dentist who is said to be "practicing" medicine or dentistry. In the same sense, however, marriage is practiced. The first observation in Scripture about marriage is a directive to be put into practice. Addressed to a man, but surely meaning a woman as well: a man shall leave his father and mother and be bonded to his wife. Unglued and glued. No directive could be plainer. It is not that we do not know enough; it is putting knowledge into practice.

This book is about putting this knowledge into practice in marriage, beginning with this need for *leaving* the old to *cleave* to the new and continuing through other specific areas of married life. In marriage there is a continuous need for forgiveness. Practicing *forgiveness* leads to *intimacy*. Forgiveness allows our hurts and irritations to be resolved in a way that leads to closeness. *Sex role conflicts* present a current challenge in practicing marriage. In this day of greater choices due to liberation from stereotypical male and female roles it is necessary that decisions be made that are satisfactory to both husband and wife for their own growth.

In times of *prosperity and adversity* the partners need to be sensitive to each other for the marriage to survive. Very few in our particular age group whom we know have been spared these adversities and even tragedies. *Cultivating companionship* has its special place in practicing marriage so that the partners do not become "married singles" in midlife. Finally, in *growing older together* practicing marriage provides the harvest of mutual thoughtfulness and concern. But it is God who gives the harvest.

The material of this book comes out of our own experience with forty years of marriage. We have known the ups and downs, the joys and sorrows, that often accompany this amazing relationship. The material also comes from our knowledge of similar experiences in other marriages. For the past decade we have been conducting workshops and retreats in spiritual and marital renewal from which we have received much insight into what helps as well as what hinders the practice of marriage.

While our approach to the practice of marriage is related to the human sciences it is basically a biblical approach. We have drawn much support for our own marriage from our biblical heritage and have witnessed its creative power in other marriages in workshop and counseling settings.

The idea for this book grew out of a series of articles giving a positive approach to marriage which we were asked to write by the editor of *Scope* magazine. The articles dealt with the young adult, midlife, and aging stages of marriage. The response was impressive and so we prepared an expansion of our ideas in this book.

We have followed the direction of the *Scope* articles and applied the practice of marriage to the various stages of life. Young readers—both married and preparing for marriage—can find themselves in these pages and see as well the way their present is related to their future. Middle-aged readers can reflect on both their past and future as they see their marriage in their own life stage. Older readers can find encouragement as they grasp the challenge of what is uniquely theirs in the maturation of their bonding. In each of these stages we have included the implications for parenthood as they apply to the practice of marriage.

"To arrive we have to take a journey." Yet arriving is a process rather than an attainment. Our faith in God helps us to take risks in achieving marital growth. In the vulnerability to which such risks expose us we are undergirded by the belief that God is *for* our marriage. It is our hope that this book will help the readers to appreciate and realize the marvelous potentials of marriage as designed by their Creator.

1

Leaving to Cleave

MARITAL WORDS OF INSTITUTION

If you are married, what do you remember from your marriage ceremony? Bill preached at our son's wedding. Our daughter-in-law remarked later that she wished she had a copy of the sermon because she could not remember much at all about the service. Perhaps you too might say that. Yet if we quoted to you the words of institution of marriage, you would probably recall their being used at your wedding. "Therefore shall a man leave his father and his mother, and shall cleave unto his wife, and they shall be one flesh." If you are not married but looking forward to marriage, you can anticipate these words in the ceremony.

Did you know that this description of the institution of marriage occurs five times in the Bible? The first instance of these words is the second account of creation, in Genesis 2. In this story, the newly created *adam* was lonely, having no partner to relate to among the creatures of the garden. Acting in compassion, the Lord took one of *adam*'s ribs while he slept and fashioned a woman who would be "a helper fit for him." When *adam* saw her, he said, "This at last is bone of my bones and flesh of my flesh." It is at that point in the account that the words appear. "Therefore a man leaves his father and his mother and cleaves to his wife, and they become one flesh" (Gen. 2:18-24).

Their use in the Gospels of Matthew and Mark was occasioned by the Pharisees' attempt to trap Jesus on the hot issue of divorce. Did he believe divorce was lawful even while Moses allowed it? Jesus' response was that what Moses had allowed was God's concession, but God's intention was in the words of institution. Jesus concluded, "So they are no longer two but one flesh. What therefore God has joined together, let no man put asunder" (Mark 10:7-9; Matt. 19:5-6).

In 1 Corinthians Saint Paul cites this description of the marital institution to voice his concern over Christians participating in the rites of mystery religions, including temple prostitution. A physical act, sexual intercourse also symbolizes a committed relationship. So, after asking, "Do you not know that he who joins himself to a prostitute becomes one body with her?" Paul justified his position with a brief reference to these words: "For it is written, 'The two shall become one flesh.'" What this means for the true worship of God follows: "But he who is united to the Lord becomes one body with him" (1 Cor. 5:16-17).

This analogy of marriage to our relationship with the Lord is the context within which these words are used in Ephesians. The apostolic writer makes the point that Christ cherishes his spouse, the church, because we (the church) are members of his body. Then he quotes the words derived from Genesis. This "one flesh" union of a man and woman in marriage, says the writer, is a profound mystery. But an even more profound mystery is the marital union of Christ with his church (Eph. 5:29-32).

These words from Genesis are the only ones from Scripture which might be read as an Old Testament lesson, a gospel lesson and two epistle lessons. This says something about the importance of marriage to the Bible's description of the human community. Marriage is described as a process of "leaving in order to cleave."

ADEQUATE OR INADEQUATE
LEAVE-TAKING

One of the most difficult processes in life is leaving father and mother. How can that be? Everybody does it—or do they? There are two distinct parts of this project: the children leave and the parents let go. In both are the seeds of trouble and joy. Like other rites of passage the wedding ceremony is only the outward side of new activity and responsibility. After our marriage ceremony an older couple, parents of a friend, said, "Just think of how much they have to learn!" At

Leaving to Cleave

the time this seemed like a criticism of our maturity. But the statement was right. Now we know from experience—especially from being parents—that people either grow or resist growth.

Parents find it difficult to realize that their children must be allowed to take whatever they have at the time of marriage and grow further. As parents we can hardly bear to see this process. We need the courage and confidence of a mother with a learning-disabled son who wrote, "Nothing for Wayne would ever be easy, but I felt a wonderful certainty that in his own time, in his own way, our son would rise to find his special place in the sun." All of us have our problems with learning. Parents and children have to learn to use their combinations of gifts to seek that special place in the sun—their maturity.

Is it any wonder that a sense of awe overcomes parents at wedding time? The sense of trusting in God may be heightened. We know that it is so hard to see that our child, not quite capable of taking the step, yet must take it—shakily—and take the responsibility for his or her decision. It is very easy for parents to blame the new partner for the disasters and take credit for the successes. It is hard not to try to protect our children from the consequences of their mistakes.

Many of us seasoned parents smile when we hear new parents sigh, "When this is over, things will be simpler." No, after each stage come new adjustments. Nowhere is this truer than in taking the step of marriage, following as it often does a period of career training, when the child is usually dependent upon the parents. The time for adjustment arrives without adequate preparation by either generation. In our culture, we expect ourselves to shift quickly from relating as parent and child to relating as friends. Is there any wonder there is confusion?

What really takes place is that parents become part of the background, rather than center stage. Why is such an elementary idea being discussed? Because in our culture we give little time to "becoming." We take the process for granted. As poet Gerhard Frost puts it, "To arrive we have to take a journey."[1] The rough roads must look smooth, and the wearing doubts as to whether we are even on the right road must not be in evidence. The newly married are afraid to fail since regressions must always bring shame.

So difficult is this transition from a relationship of power and dependence to friendship that some cultures do not even attempt it. Young people remain as powerless as children until their own offspring are married. Lucy teaches in a community college which has many international students. The two desires they most frequently express for their own lives are to enter a monogamous marriage and to establish a home separate from their parents. These students want a separate home so badly because they often do not have the opportunity in their present family setting to make their own mistakes. Their description of the squabbles and resentments at home, which waste precious creative energy, is very vivid.

If we ignore the need to form a friendship with our parents, and if we do not come to a satisfying relationship with the parents of our mate and other family members, an ache comes into our soul. In some way this disappointment spoils other relationships. No wonder some societies prefer to leave the power with the older generation. When there is so little in our culture to indicate how changes in relationships are to be accomplished, dissatisfaction can be expected. These adjustments are very difficult to bring about. It should not surprise us that husbands become entangled in their mother's apron strings and wives in the role of Daddy's little girl. Knowing that these are unacceptable ways to adjust may do nothing more than ensure they will operate unconsciously. It is so much easier to deny the challenges than go through the messy process of growth. In our picture of ourselves we need to have a place for growth—for practicing marriage.

UNFINISHED BUSINESS

Our growth in intimacy and friendship in marriage is a benefit to the larger community. Men and women who are intentionally creating satisfactory connections between intimates are free to be helpful and have good will to others. They will tend to apply that same energy and openness to growth in all other relationships. We are poor indeed if we have never witnessed the effect of a loving couple's affection on their surroundings. It blesses all that it touches. They have understood the effort that good relationships require, and desire also to relate more intentionally to others. They care. On the other hand, persons locked into patterns of powerlessness or who are confused about these primary relationships do not allow themselves to be of good will to others. Unresolved conflicts all too often become displaced upon others who have no connection with the source of conflict. Have you ever been caught in a battle that you realized had nothing to do with you, but with other troubled relationships?

Leaving to Cleave

Parents, unless they know their shadow side, their weaknesses, faults, and fears, may place their own unresolved conflicts in the new couple's way. It is hard to accept profound changes. In one of the most impressive wedding ceremonies that we have seen, the officiating clergywoman asked the parents to promise to do nothing that could possibly work against the new couple becoming a functioning unit. Perhaps this innovation ought to become part of all church wedding ceremonies.

When a marriage is slipping into trouble, the difficult task of children leaving father and mother and of father and mother letting go is one of the first places to look for the root of the conflict. Conflict may be the result of not grappling with the issues of independence and responsibility. It is to be expected more often than not that all members of the family will have some difficulty adjusting. And a healthy recognition of this fact can be very freeing. Many of the situations which demand adjustment do not arise before the occasion of marriage. A willingness to approach the problem without denial and blame will help us in dealing with conflict.

Never is trouble more imminent than when everybody is sure there will be none. But because our images of love have been so conditioned by the media, we may have unrealistic ideas of what is possible. Seldom do we see any models for working long-term with a difficult problem. A bitter woman put it like this: "When my husband and I had a conflict, I was taken out for dinner." In other words, there was no attempt to deal with the conflict. When families have conflicts, their first reaction may be to deny the conflict rather than grapple with it. A man may subtly deny his wife's claim on him and continue to placate his mother; a woman may be unwilling to claim her new power if she sees it as a threat to her relationship with her father. Both are denying the new relationship. To many, working through a problem with nonmaterial solutions is a new creative experience.

Especially since the rise of the psychoanalytic theory of personality development, it is handy to blame problems on one's parents. Relationships are not enhanced by blaming, however. All that blaming produces is defensiveness. What is needed is to face the conflict so that forgiveness can take place. In a values-clarification workshop, Sid Simon used an exercise that may help overcome this tendency to blame our parents. He had the participants say in unison, "No matter what they did, they did the best they could."

Considering the limitations of our parents, what they were given or not given, they may have done remarkably well! Even so, have they—or we ourselves—really done the best we could? Probably not. More likely, we let our self-centeredness, our need to retaliate, or our defensiveness get in the way. We know we could have done otherwise. Could we not have responded instead to the Spirit's direction and done things differently? If this is true for us it is probably also true for our parents. So on what basis can we accept them? On the basis of forgiveness! This is the forgiveness that comes from God to us, which we can extend to our parents.

One of the things that blocks us from growing together is our unwillingness to face the hostility that may be present. Hostility is especially hard to see when its outward signs are hidden. The new relationships, for example, may provoke jealousy. The old relationships are threatened as power and influence are redistributed. Parents may show hostility by "telling tales out of school"—those unflattering tales of one's youth. A new marriage also reminds the older generation of the shortness and limitedness of their future. The joy and happiness of the new couple may shed some light into dark corners of their lives, perhaps revealing how their own marriage has deteriorated.

While it is difficult to admit that a much loved parent or sibling can be hostile, or that children may fall into the easy route of blaming others for their troubles, it is better to admit to these problems. Only when the present and past feelings of hostility are recognized and dealt with openly can the relationship grow. The worst advice that can be taken is that one should "forget it." No, rather forgive it. Forgiveness is an act which takes effort.

At one of our family reunions we children of our parents, now grandparents and great-grandparents ourselves, talked much about our parents. We are not a family that can easily confront one another or for that matter easily verbalize our feelings. We talked about our parents and how we saw their strengths and weaknesses. There was much difference of opinion. Parents do not look the same to those who have a ten-year difference in age. There was criticism, of course. Yet if we could not forgive them, we could not go on to appreciate their strengths. There is something terribly sad about mulling over past hurts at an advanced age rather than forgiving them. May our children discover our strengths by forgiving our failures and taking a clearheaded look at our parenting. Then we will be worthy of "They did the best they could!" The wisdom of forgiving is the power in all relationships. How beautiful it is when relatives become friends.

Today it is not uncommon for families to have grown children a continent away. The notion that parents can influence them daily or know what is happening to them has to go. When our daughter lived in Mexico, a two-week wait for a letter was very different from a similar wait to hear from busy in-town children. Mobility can be helpful in letting go. In addition, very few of us ever repeat the patterns of our parents' lives. My mother, for example, left a cozy small town to become an isolated farm wife; I left that farm to live in a big city. None of our children is living a life similar to ours. Parental expectations of what children's lives should be like have to be relinquished. Since ours is the only life we know, these expectations are very deep. During children's formative years, parents must have expectations of them. When they marry, these expectations will need to be modified; now the children choose their own course. Is it so hard to see that this would be an area where tact and patience and trust are required? Parental expectations are out of line when parents dictate to their grown children. The best a parent can do is to become a true friend, a friend who believes that the marriage and careers of their children are proceeding in a positive direction. Their setbacks and regressions will be their opportunity for growth. Theirs will be a wonderful story, filled with unique adventures. Every couple needs encouragement and not a laundry list of fears. These fears more often than not represent a list of the parents' own fears. For example, when I was teaching a daughter to make pie crust, at the point of putting it in the pan I called out, "Be careful." "But Mom, it is already in the pan!" The fear was mine; her problems were not mine.

THE REALITY TEST FOR LEAVING

If children are added to the adjustment of marriage a very complex process is set in motion in which the leaving process becomes even more important. The new adjustment operates the same whether the couple is in their teens or thirties. We are very romantic about babies. We have many cultural expectations about what they will do for us, but our reactions are not predictable. When we become parents we may be surprised by the new facets in the family system. Some find that they become parents or grandparents reluctantly. They could not have predicted their own feelings.

Strangely enough, being able to accept our own childhood becomes important now. Without our knowing it, our own childhood comes into our awareness every time we look at the new child. Old dreams of perfection—concerning physical appearance and social behavior, for example—may get in our way. Ultimately these idealized dreams put too much burden on the child. We need to accept (forgive) our own childhood so we can accept the child's.

The new adjustments put the people whose relationship is vital to the baby in a vulnerable position. The successful, educated people in our culture may never have been faced with a problem which seems to be insoluble. Babies can make us feel very insecure. The new grandparents may take this vulnerability as a cue to reassert their authority. Old conflicts and dependencies can then reoccur. The new parents may be uncomfortable in asking for advice. Grandparents may be upset if their advice is not taken.

The grandparents have the need to be honestly valued as resources for the new child. If the leave-taking that is involved in marriage has not been adequate, this new relationship between the new parents and their parents can be on shaky ground. Unresolved conflicts, especially if they were put on hold to keep peace, may come back with renewed vigor. There is simply not the energy to keep unresolved conflicts buried. If either generation withdraws, the relationships deteriorate. These are challenging and potentially rewarding times! The goal is for all to grow emotionally so that satisfaction and joy are derived from the process.

The complexities of this leaving process are best dealt with by joining some other parents who are making the same adjustments. Social support and helpful information can be exchanged, and unexpected difficulties aired. The information received is invaluable for our own creative thinking for the uniqueness of our child. We need to know how other families function so that we are not confined to the limited input of our own family patterns. Dealing with this need for learning sets us on the course for positive parenting. Sometimes one's partner may be too defensive or confused to be of much help in these matters and may not even want to deal with the issue, let alone see it as important. The fear that one may have harmed one's child irreparably triggers emotions that threaten us with depression. Yet our peers in the same boat can supply invaluable help. But we need to develop the character and will to use new insights.

BECOMING ONE FLESH

After the leaving, there is the cleaving—when the two, wife and husband, become *one flesh*. What does "one flesh" mean? Obviously those who are married are still two distinct individuals with two different bodies. Yet they join their bodies in sexual intercourse and symbolically become one in that experience. Flesh in this context, however, means more than body, though it includes the body. One flesh means *one life together*—that wife and husband have become one unit in human society. Theirs is a relationship that is more than just two people living and doing things together. In addition they have committed themselves to share their life together totally, to meet life with all of its challenges and problems together. Through this union they have the potential to be bearers and rearers of new life together.

How do you take two unique persons—different not only physically but intellectually and socially—and form them into a unit in which each retains their own identity? We all have our rough edges; we are not smoothly ground pebbles. When our edges do not fit with our mate's edges, we both experience pain as we move toward each other. We may then withdraw from each other because of this pain. Becoming one flesh is the process of learning to fit together, each with the other's edges.

Couples rarely perceive this process as gradual and consistent. This is the way a tree or a plant grows, but it is not the way people or relationships grow. There may be times when it seems like the relationship is going backward, but this is also a part of the process. Becoming one flesh is a lifetime pursuit—a lifetime of practicing marriage.

By its very nature the process of becoming one flesh requires forsaking all others—as the wedding vows state. Perhaps it is easier for some to do this than for others. When we were growing up many of the novels that we read stressed the folly of choosing a mate primarily on the basis of sexual attraction. Today's popular literature gives the *fantasy* that making a choice does not eliminate other choices. Contemporary literature seldom serves as a model for real consequences of faulty judgment. Nor does it serve as a viable model for a marriage in which mutually exclusive choices can be seen as both workable and exciting.

This is what our friends meant when they said we had so much to learn. They were a couple who had lived out the forsaking of others. They had gained from this giving up. What is gained is an intense intimate relationship for which humans yearn. Without making that choice, our energies can never be concentrated upon one goal. This concentration of our energies upon a single relationship is one way to learn who we are. Giving up to get in this way gives us a start on the most creative venture open to humanity.

Forsaking all others is a discipline behind the process of marriage. We accept this discipline when we decide to get married. The discipline is simply our living our marital commitment—our practicing marriage. Forsaking all others is not a discipline parents expect of their children. It is a distinctively adult potential. This is why marriage is for adults—those who are mature enough to have left father and mother.

As adults, however, all of us still have our "child" within us. This child is often attractive to others. But this does not mean that the inner child is necessarily dependable. He or she can be a lot of fun, but responsibility is a quality into which children grow as they mature. Then too, some children turn out not to be so attractive. They move us to want to shake them rather than hug them. Often, this is the way we feel toward "the child within us"—though others may view our "child" differently.

As an adult function, the discipline of forsaking all others—of giving up to get—is based on our priorities and loyalties. These priorities and loyalties reveal our "character"—who we really are. Our character comes to the fore when we have to make a choice. Otherwise we can remain uncommitted and concealed.

Leaving to cleave, therefore, means not only leaving parents but also other lovers. In the film *Three Approaches to Psychotherapy*, psychotherapist Carl Rogers is counseling with Gloria. Gloria complains that she wants to be free to violate her own sexual morality without feeling guilty. She also wants to be honest with her daughter about her conduct without losing her daughter's respect. Rogers says, "That's a big order!" It is so big an order that it cannot be done. If we persistently violate the principles we respect, we are behaving destructively toward ourselves and toward those we care about.

Some individuals seem constitutionally incapable of fidelity to their spouse. Forsaking all others, giving up to get, appears to be beyond their ability. When there is opportunity and physical attraction, how can it be turned down? This, however, is the way a child's mind operates. In the area of sex, such persons are still children. Historians love these characters, as do novelists and dramatists. The child approach to sex among these adults fascinates us. Their adventures make good stories.

Rather than looking at this behavior pattern as a flaw in their character, however, we tend to view it as the mark of a *colorful* character. Lesley Darmen expresses this attraction to the "bad child" in her article, "Bring Back the Bad Girls." She says she is bored with the portrayal of good wives in the media. "Whatever happened," she asks, "to the *femme fatale?*" The "sexually exploitive, good-time bad girl" lets the reader, the viewer, indulge her own "secret bad-girl fantasies." Her conclusion: "We need bad girls. Through them we are reckless heartbreakers and lust-inspiring viragoes."[2]

As Darmen freely admits, our attraction to the sexually promiscuous does not fit well with our supposed respect for sexual morality. This double-mindedness over temptation leads to double signals, which in turn can lead to double living. Or perhaps it merely leads to a vicarious living out of this darker part of ourselves. Parents can give such double signals to their children. They tell them to behave but in such a way that the child gets the message that they really like boys who are little rascals and girls who are colorful and provocative.

The fact remains, however, that unfaithfulness in marriage undermines relationships and, ultimately, undermines community. Both depend on openness and trust. If the "colorful" characteristics of the "attractive child" in these adults were the general pattern of our populace, we simply could not survive as a society. If we faced up to our own double-mindedness about using sex without commitment, we might see this as a flaw even in an otherwise adult character.

AN APPROACH TO OUR DIFFERENCES

What if our edges prove to be too sharp to cleave together and produce so much pain in the attempt that we become discouraged? "We are just two different people and it hasn't worked," is the way one discouraged wife put it. Yet it is not differences alone that disrupt a marriage, but the way these differences are perceived in the relationship.

Differences are also potentially enriching. They need not overshadow our common humanity, nor our common faith.

We may be attracted, subconsciously at least, to those who are different than we are. None of us is a complete human being in terms of possessing all of the qualities of the human potential. Differences, like gifts, are distributed rather than concentrated. We are all gifted by the Giver. When we say someone is "gifted," what do we mean? Usually that the person is gifted in a particular way—mentally, artistically, athletically. But who is to say that these are the "higher gifts"? Our culture, perhaps. Yet, our culture is only one among many cultures—all of them evaluating gifts differently—and it is obviously biased in favor of some gifts over others.

We rarely rate our own gifts as highly as the gifts we see in others, gifts we feel we are lacking. Cultural differences, religious differences, social differences are cases in point. We are frequently attracted to what we ourselves did not grow up with—at the same time downplaying the value of what we did grow up with. We need exposure to these differences but we cannot possess them all ourselves.

Those whose difference from us we find attractive may be easier to date than to live with. Often the personal qualities that we find attractive are not the qualities that build enduring relationships. Also, our attraction to qualities differing from those we possess may contain a hidden rejection of these qualities, even as an overt rejection of differences may mask a hidden attraction. The tendency to depreciate those who are different from us, and to assume that our way or our kind is best, may be stronger than our attraction to differences.

While much is made of opposites attracting each other, social scientists believe differently, namely, that *similarities* attract. The general public, however, gives credence to the common observation: "They don't get along because they are just too much alike." Like differences, similarities can be attractive but troublesome. How, for example, do two dominating personalities form a one-flesh relationship? A dominating person married to a submissive person may seem a better fit; yet this mix may be destructive to a genuine union of two persons. The one-flesh relationship should be a stimulant to the growth of each of the partners. But in this case the one partner dominates the other; the relationship stymies rather than stimulates the growth of the partners as each becomes more fixed in his or her own personality deficiencies.

Though similarities in education, race, religion, ethnic background,

Leaving to Cleave

and socioeconomic status may attract people to each other, differences are also present. No two people come from identical families of origin, or from similar positions in their families of origin. Psychologist David Buss—who has surveyed a mass of social science papers and conducted his own research on mate selection to substantiate his position that people are more likely to marry those similar to themselves—is himself an example of this difference within similarities in his own marriage. Although he and his wife are similar in almost every way, they are quite different, he says, in terms of self-disclosure. His wife is open about revealing what is going on within her and he is not.[3] As any marriage counselor knows this is a whopping difference, and a major problem area for marriages.

Other differences may stem from our family background: male and female roles, patterns in child rearing, ways of dealing with conflict, personal interests and concerns. Marriage counselor Hugh Misseldine illustrates the impact of our families of origin on marriage as the four people who have to learn to fit in the same marriage bed—the mates plus both mates' inner child of the past.[4] By implication this makes six in the bed since our parents go with our inner child. We do marry our partner's family!

How we interpret our differences is the key to the role they play in our marriage. If we compare our differences in terms of good or bad, better or worse, we are making value judgments that obstruct our acceptance. Differences need first to be accepted before they can be enriching. So if we simply describe our differences rather than evaluate them, we will be moving in the right direction. Then the learning that comes with living together will allow us to synthesize these differences in our marriage. One flesh, then, becomes a distinct mix—a beautiful potential.

Jack and Jane are an example of a couple who went from judging to accepting their differences. They came from very different families even though they were of the same religious, ethnic, and socioeconomic background. Jack's family was not family-centered. Each did his or her own thing. In Jane's family, the family did things together. Jack's family rarely took vacations, and when they did, the parents vacationed alone. In Jane's family, family vacations were a top priority. Friends were family friends. In Jack's family, friends were made on an individual basis.

When the children arrived, the differences between Jack and Jane became more evident. The differences became a source of pain. As all too often happens, they responded to this pain by simply going their separate ways. Jane devoted herself to her children and Jack devoted himself to his work. Both realized what was happening to their marriage, but neither could deal with the problem directly. Jack did not because he feared conflict, and whenever it erupted he would run angrily away. His skills were manual rather than verbal and he withdrew. Jane did not deal with the problem because she felt insecure in the relationship and did not want to jeopardize it. Longing for the companionship that went with his ideal of marriage, Jack found it in another woman. Jane felt betrayed and cheated. Jack felt misunderstood and cheated by Jane's preoccupation with their children.

This crisis in their relationship forced them both to deal with their differences. Realizing that they live in a fallen world and that they are fallen people, and consequently cannot have a perfect marriage, they are searching for the best possible, imperfect marriage. In the process they are learning to appreciate the differences between them that they previously disparaged. They are finding that these differences provide the opportunity for balance rather than for dissension. Partners with differing personal qualities and images of family life, like Jack and Jane, do not need to pull in the opposite directions. They can pull together in the search for an enriching balance in their becoming one flesh.

A good way to see what the situation is regarding differences in *your* relationship is to do the following exercise: First, make separate lists of the differences between you as each perceives them, place a plus or minus beside each difference to distinguish those that appear to enrich the relationship and those that remain obstacles. Then share your lists with each other. Do not get defensive; rather listen and learn how your partner feels. Then brainstorm together on how the minuses could be changed into pluses. Select the most feasible of the generated ideas and mutually go to work on them. Set a time to evaluate your progress.

2

Through Forgiveness to Intimacy

Practicing marriage is a practice in intimate living. Intimacy—closeness with another—brings deep satisfaction to the human spirit. Intimacy eases the anxiety of our estrangement and loneliness. We feel *joined* to another, and it feels warm and good. We have found our "fit" and feel completed. The Creator said, "It is not good that the man should be alone" (Gen. 2:24). The answer to human loneliness—whether man's or woman's—includes marriage but also goes beyond marriage to include the human community of supportive friendships.

INTIMACY BRINGS SATISFACTION

Intimacy is obviously something for which we were made. While many human attributes are associated with being created in the divine image, the biblical emphasis is on intimacy. Being created in God's image means being created for communion with God. This union is what distinguishes our humanity and completes it.

Following the institution of marriage in Genesis is the story of the Fall. The Fall is a fall away from the divine image—from communion into isolation, alienation, and loneliness. The Creator's act of redeeming fallen humanity restores it to communion—to intimacy. All the barriers to closeness are removed through the divine initiative of forgiveness. This forgiveness is received in the initiatory sacrament of baptism in which we are covenanted, bonded to God, in a union that is comparable to marriage.

This bonding is more than a verbal covenant of forgiveness. We are *loved*, and forgiveness is an expression of this love. God's love is tangible—symbolized by the tangible water of baptism. God has incarnated love, *enfleshed* it. God became one of us in Christ to love us in a human way. The word commonly used for the tangible expression of love is "affection." We are loved in our bodies and through our bodies. We are *touched* by love. In the one-flesh relationship, the sexual intimacy of marriage is the epitome of this touch.

Communion means communication. Intimacy is also a union of minds. Marital partners are soul mates. Analogous to our communion with God, "one flesh" signifies a union of body and mind and spirit, with sexual intercourse as its most holistic expression.

THE PAINS OF INTIMACY

Intimacy, for all of its joys, also brings hurt. It can reveal our worst as well as our best. Therefore we fear intimacy even as we long for it. There is a risk in uniting with another—you can get hurt.

Why should closeness hurt us? Because in our humanity we can fall into destructive attitudes and behavior toward each other. First of all, we can become *careless*. Philosopher Edgar Shefield Brightman used to say to us students that carelessness was the initial phase of sinning. Perhaps you have noted how you can be more careful and considerate with people whose care for you is conditional than you are with your spouse. These people "keep us on our toes" in order to keep us on their good side, while our partner is supposed to accept our neglect.

In being careless we also become insensitive. Preoccupied with our own feelings and thoughts we fail to sense our partner's feelings and thoughts. So we become inconsiderate because we are oblivious to our partner's needs.

We can even be aware of our partner's needs and still be inconsiderate, due to our tendency to arrogance. Of course, it is to be expected that the very nature of "close" living will produce its irritations. The critical issue is how we *deal* with them. Often we do not deal with irritations very well. Either we suppress our feelings, which then come out indirectly, or we vent them in a direct attack on our partner. In either case we become resentful and this affects our relationship, changing us from lovers into judges. Our attitude is "I'm right; you're wrong!"

The wounds that these destructive tendencies produce occur at a very deep level in the human spirit because they occur in the one-flesh

Through Forgiveness to Intimacy

relationship. Our spirits are as naked in this union as our bodies in sexual intercourse. We are vulnerable because in so exposing and giving of ourselves we have trusted one another. To be then taken for granted, treated inconsiderately, or judged in an arrogant way leaves a deep hurt.

Behind the anger, hostility, and even hatred that can characterize traumatic times in a marriage is hurt. The opposite of love is not hostility or hatred, but apathy and indifference. As every marriage counselor knows, there is more hope for a troubled marriage when the partners care enough about each other to fight—and even hate—than when they "couldn't care less." These violent feelings occur primarily because of a rupture in the deep commitment of love. It is our experience from counseling that when one partner is hurt, both are hurt. Yet each is usually likely to feel only his or her own pain. "My husband (wife) cannot possibly be hurt as badly as I am. Nor can they be as justified as I am in feeling hurt. My spirit is raw with pain. It feels *bruised* like a bruised body."

In spite of the seeming hellishness of the hurts that are possible in marital intimacy, marriage remains an institution created by God. A question was once raised at a marriage enrichment retreat about what is distinctively Christian in marriage. The answer was, *nothing!* Although instituted by God and analogous to the Christian's relationship with God, marriage belongs to the whole human family—including Muslims and Hindus, atheists and agnostics. Yet there is a distinctly Christian *contribution* to marriage in the Christian perspective of marriage as a paradigm of our communion with God.

Our "marriage" to God is a covenant based on reconciliation. Reconciliation is precisely what is needed in the hurts of marital intimacy. God's self-giving love is the bond of the covenant. This same love can be reflected in the human union. Our bonding with God based on reconciling love provides us with the security of soul we need to deal healthily with conflict in marriage. Such conflicts also occur in our marriage with God. Who has not at least inwardly protested what seemed to be a perverseness in providence, or quarreled with God over what went wrong in our lives? Yet the bond remained firm. Nothing—not even our quarreling with God—can separate us from God's love, for it is *unconditional*.

So also with our human marriage. The bond can hold even when wounds are inflicted through carelessness, insensitivity, arrogance, and sometimes even retaliation. Why? Because we have a prior marriage in our baptism in which we are bonded by unconditional love and reconciling forgiveness. We can give to our human marriage the acceptance we have received from our divine marriage. It is our base of security for practicing marriage.

ACCEPTANCE AND RESIGNATION

The Serenity Prayer of Alcoholics Anonymous expresses this concept of acceptance. "God grant me the serenity to accept things I cannot change, courage to change things I can, and wisdom to know the difference." Accepting reality is the opposite of denying it. We do not believe that acceptance means being resigned to something. Rather we believe it is the first step toward forgiveness. Acceptance is an act of love. To accept another, and what that one does, is to pay close attention. This kind of acceptance begins with our becoming aware of what is going on in the relationship. Forgiveness without this step of acceptance is not true forgiveness. The commitment to follow Christ is to take action rather than to be passive. To act, we first need to be aware of and present to our environment or, as Henri Nouwen says, to become present to ourselves.[1]

Our preformed ideas have to be open to challenge by every new situation. Bored people and boring people take refuge in clichés: "Isn't that just like a man!"; "Just like a woman!" We take comfort in these sayings, being deluded into thinking we know something. After hearing a clear case of sexual harassment in his office, an executive said, "Boys will be boys." Clearly that executive did not want to be aware of the victim. He did not want to admit to knowing what was going on.

An attitude of resignation, in contrast to acceptance, is a rejection of the other or of the present moment. *Resignation* is withdrawal from others. In a marriage when a couple is resigned to each other, they neither look closely at the other nor pay close attention to what is going on in the home; often the conversation falls back into judgments like "You always do that"; "You'll never change!"

Acceptance in its active form results in forgiveness. We cannot assume we have forgiven just by saying that it is so. All too often in a marriage relationship we have become resigned to hurtful behavior instead of being accepting and forgiving. Our carelessness lets us think

Through Forgiveness to Intimacy

that we are attuned to each other when we are only used to each other. When one is committed to forgiving as he or she has been forgiven, the actions in the marriage need to lead to that end. Admittedly, it is hard to take the initiative. Lethargy may have to be overcome.

It may seem easier to ignore boorish behavior in our mate or to become incapable of reacting to it with straight messages because of our laziness disguised as powerlessness. Sometimes, in the company of others, we may ignore the mate's inconsiderate behavior. Rather than ignoring the situation, fearing embarrassment, the partner needs to accept what is going on. The social situation has already been disrupted. Then the response can be direct. "That is not helpful," or "That hurts."

In any conflict, if one can be objective enough to stay in the "adult" stage, then one can ask, "What bothers me about this situation?" Feelings are not strictly rational; however, there is a reason behind all feelings. We need to respect our feelings and to acknowledge them.

Some challenges from others are in order; other challenges represent a power play from one who cannot pass up the sight of another's vulnerability. Just to be aware of what is going on is a responsible action. Yet we can become depressed when we become conscious of our part in the interaction if we do not take appropriate action. Sometimes the child in us, for example, would rather think that others are out to hurt us. When we do not see this tendency objectively, we can get into a muddled quarrel with someone else's childish state. The possibility is multiplied if either partner is in a sensitive state due to factors such as physical problems or stress outside the home.

Only after close observation of what is going on and the identification of feelings can forgiveness begin. Only after that comes forgetting. So the words "forgive and forget" are often spoken together. If one cannot forget, it may be because forgiveness has been confused with resignation and its lack of respect for the other person. True forgetting is the simple process of letting information no longer needed slip away. Information passes out of consciousness either by repression or because there is no further need for it. Once a conflict is resolved, it does not matter whether it is forgotten or not. The power is taken from it. Some painful images, however, may always remain with us.

We question the advice so often given at any difficulty: "Try to forget it." This *trying* means spending energy on a task which yields no return. A real return comes with working the problem through to forgiveness. Saint Paul said that we become a new creation through reconciliation (2 Cor. 5:17). Through forgiveness we become new, and we need to become acquainted with the new person. Forgetting means "letting the old pass away," so that "the new can come." Obviously, careful attention to forgiveness is necessary all through married life. It is basic to practicing marriage.

It is a continual challenge to be open with our mates and ourselves so that we can share our hurts. All of marriage is an intense learning laboratory. Dan Kiley describes resistance to becoming an adult as the Peter Pan Syndrome. One of his tests for this syndrome is: "Never wants to say, 'I'm sorry.' " To say "I'm sorry" means to grow, and the hallmark of Peter Pan is to stay the child. The adult stage is characterized by the awareness of another's pain which we caused, as well as our own pain which we have received from another. Only in the fantasy world do these pains not happen. Kiley further asserts that in our culture we also have a Wendy Complex. For every Peter there is a Wendy ready to rescue. Wendy helps Peter deny and forget the pain rather than cope with reality and ask for forgiveness.[2]

So strongly does psychiatrist Scott Peck feel about growth in marriage that he says that husband and wife are responsible for each other's spiritual growth.[3] Perhaps some may believe Peck is asking too much; however, if we have been serious about practicing marriage we can see that by accepting and forgiving, we do hold the power for growth in our working together. Through forgiveness we become new together.

TOO HURT FOR RECONCILIATION?

There are times when each mate will be tempted to feel too hurt or too discouraged about the relationship to be reconciled. A despondency takes over our feelings about the relationship. There may be several reasons for this. We may have developed a habit of discouragement rather than hope—a lack of faith that all eventually will work out. Another reason may lie in having a faulty perception of marriage. One who loves us, we say, will not hurt us. In this case, we are expecting mates to be protective parents to us. While there will always be some aspect of parenting in the relationship of marriage, unconditional love is an unattainable ideal. Real people do hurt those whom they love. The cultural conditioning of our Puritan heritage teaches us to reject imperfect things. The idea of mending the imperfect comes tardily to our minds.

A study of American Lutheran Church women revealed that the women over 60 were often depressed and angry. These women, our contemporaries, were ill-equipped by our culture to deal with hurt and anger. Anger is an emotion that was stuffed into the subconscious only to erupt when one was off guard. Finally, with fewer distractions in their later years, anger over hurts is being expressed. Yet they lack the skills to deal with anger or even to identify it within them.[4]

Many of the hurts in marriage are not intentional, yet poor communication skills add to the pain. They make it difficult to distinguish between a power struggle and an honest disagreement of principles. The culture we live in is of little help, since it emphasizes individuality over cooperation. In this sense our culture works against the process of marriage—a blending of two people.

The sheer abundance of our material wealth and opportunities provides us with many options, options which call for decisions, and decisions which call for marital partners to cooperate. Decisions can open the door to many hurts and misunderstandings. One of Lucy's Third World students once said: "There are just too many choices to make here; no wonder people do not stay married." She helped us see a very important possibility for innocent hurting.

Resentment over restrictive sex roles has given way to increased choices concerning career and motherhood for today's women. Yet, we have not adjusted to these social changes. There are many casualties. The demand for child care is only partially met. The bride who balanced homemaking and even child rearing with a career and economic hardship can be very hurt when her husband abandons her after that stint is over. Since men are now freed from the need to swallow all emotions, they too can rail over the seeming unfairness of having to succeed in a vocation and do half of the housework. Nevertheless, we have high hopes for the couples of today who are practicing marriage without models. They have been better trained to express their hurts and anger.

Marriage counselor George Bach has developed new communication skills which will do a better job of dealing with the impasses and discouragement in marriages in the face of hurt and anger.[5] Bach has couples make direct statements to each other about their feelings. The one addressed restates the other's words exactly as they were given.

Approximately will not do! We have participated in this exercise and know the difficulty of not adding or leaving something out. However difficult, being present to one's mate to understand what he or she is feeling can do wonders. It feels like a gift. Without such listening, communication will remain muddied. If there is no listening, there is no practicing marriage. A habitual lack of listening on the part of either partner will kill a marriage.

One of the most common reactions to hurt and anger is the silent treatment. Probably it is a sign of not having left father and mother. As children most of us used it. In small families its effect was dramatic. Others in the family became anxious. In large families, the dramatic sense was probably lost, but one could still turn inward in self-justification.

Carried into marriage, the silent treatment is damaging. The target is supposed to be an equal. The punishment implied in the silent treatment will come back on oneself. The partner at whom the silence is directed will seldom respond like a concerned parent. It may provoke a judgmental stereotype: "You are too awful to deal with," or "You don't understand." Whereas parents eventually restore peace in a family, there is no parent in this situation to do this—unless one of the partners is a Wendy rescuer, in which case there is no peer relationship.

The silent treatment puts the relationship on hold. Yet no relationship can be put on hold: the vacuum will be filled with negative feelings. Unless there is speaking, neither partner will know the nature of the hurts or how they were caused.

Anger is a feeling to which we need to apply wisdom. There is so much variation in anger's strength, duration, and expression that it is doubtful if any couple who are present to each other ever get over being surprised by it. Anger is caused by certain stresses or provocations. Although anger is a natural response to frustration, annoyance, abuse, and injustice, very few of us like to have it expressed. That is because few of us learn early enough to express anger without making a direct or indirect personal attack.

Lucy was like many women who learned to control anger until it broke forth in what Bach calls a "Vesuvius."[6] He feels that such explosions are healthy. That was a refreshing idea since these occurrences had always brought shame. But a Vesuvius finally brings up the repressed thoughts that have long been controlled and that have controlled us. In our wedding sermon the pastor in 1945 took issue with a popular article of the day entitled, "Have a Good Quarrel." To him it was "considerable nonsense." We quarreled nevertheless. What we have since learned is to express our anger to the provocations *as they occur*. Anger repressed too long, particularly when combined with the silent treatment, is almost certain to become destructive.

HELP FROM GOD TO FORGIVE

Our marriage to Christ is more than an inner union of his Spirit with our spirit, a personal bonding or dialogue. Rather this marriage has a corporate dimension as well. The *church* is the *bride* of Christ. It is also the *body* of Christ. The interrelationship of the members of this body provides the social complement to the inner dialogue of the individual with Christ. The body of Christ is a community of faith and is realized most concretely in the local congregation, and in groups that gather to support each other in their common hope and faith.

The body of Christ—wherever and however it is localized in our midst—offers us the support system of *friends*. God is referred to as our friend in both testaments, and Jesus specifically called his followers friends rather than servants. Friendship is thus a privileged, selective, and intimate relationship which is included also in the marital relationship. Married people, among other things, should be good friends. As we have noted, a primal reason for the institution of marriage in the Genesis story was the loneliness of *adam*. God provided a helpmeet, a companion. Marital companions can be supported in their friendship by friendships with their fellow members in the body of Christ.

In this body of Christ, the reconciliation that comes through Christ is lived out in the human community. We gather together as Christ's body to celebrate our relationships to God, namely, to *worship*. In this community of faith the abstract nature of forgiveness as a doctrine of the church becomes concrete in the experience of reconciliation in the fellowship of the church. Even as the human Jesus revealed to us the Divinity, so also the human community of faith reveals to us the risen Christ. Words take hold for us when they describe what we are experiencing. The ministry of the members to each other in the body is a ministry of acceptance.

Unfortunately this social acceptance by the body of its members is not always realized in this or that congregation. Sometimes the opposite—judgment and rejection—is more characteristic. Yet the divine potential is still present in the midst of human pathology. Someone—perhaps you—needs to take the initiative to restore the congregation to its covenant of forgiveness, the covenant that makes it unique among social institutions. As we receive forgiveness, we can give it.

In fact, we can give only what we have received. Otherwise our "giving" will be an outer act contaminated by inner resistance. When the "righteous one" does the forgiving, it is deadly for marriage. Such "forgiving" is without the mutuality of two becoming one flesh—there is no hugging and kissing. In the place of affection there is a reserved and restrained giving that says in effect, "You ought to be grateful. Look how far I'm bending—from the heights of innocence to the depths of the guilty."

In a sermon on the story of the "sinful" woman who was criticized for anointing Jesus' feet with both a precious perfume and her tears, theologian Paul Tillich says, "The righteous too want forgiveness, but they believe they do not need much of it. And so their righteous actions are warmed by very little love."[7] Referring to the woman he said, "It is *not* the love of the woman that brings her forgiveness, but it is the forgiveness she has received that creates her love."[8] Those who have received forgiveness are like this woman who anointed Jesus' feet in gratitude. They give—even forgiveness—with much affection.

Forgiveness allows our hurts from the inevitable results of provocation and anger and even attack to be forgotten. In this way a greater intimacy results rather than a distancing—a softening rather than a hardening of the heart. When we do not allow ourselves to escape into seclusion nor from each other's true emotions, we become aware of our own need for forgiveness: we see the logs in our own eyes. The prayer to forgive as we have been forgiven makes us squirm. God has given us the responsibility for our own souls.

Fiction writer and essayist Katherine Anne Porter, in a personalized essay about marriage, describes the audacious nature of this responsibility. "When she spoke a vow to love and honor her husband until death, she did a very reckless thing, for it is not possible by an act of the will to fulfill such an engagement. But it is the necessary act of faith performed in defense of a mode of feeling, the statement of honorable intention to practice as well as she is able the noble acquired faculty of love, that very mysterious overtone to sex, which is the best thing in it."[9]

The normal slipping of any relationship when one's dark side is snagged provides an opportunity to deal with this part of us which may have been previously unrecognized. Again, Katherine Anne Porter: "She is dismayed, horrified, full of guilt and forebodings because she is finding out little by little that she is capable of hating her husband, whom she loves faithfully."[10] It is not a time to sink into despair. All of us have this capacity to hate. Counselors, teachers, psychiatrists, and clergy, although they can help others, can be as unaware of their own repressed feelings as anyone else, and as surprised when they come into consciousness. All are under the divine directive to forgive as they have been forgiven. This is why one who has been forgiven much can love much. That person has also lived *more*.

When we examine the process of forgiveness we understand love better. "Love hopes all things," and lives in the hope that learning is taking place (1 Cor. 13:7). There is really little time for boredom when we live in forgiveness. It is hard to feel love when we feel manipulated or impulsively attacked. (A controlling person is trying in this way to be secure and an impulsive person is really trying to overcome fear.) We find it difficult to cope with our own fear and insecurity, let alone that of our mate. Yet there is no good alternative. Through recognizing our own feelings and dealing with them we become able to say, "I am sorry; please forgive me." It is our best chance of becoming one flesh in the context of hope.

A GOOD CLOSURE

This reaching out to the other in forgiveness makes possible a good closure to the day. We need a closure which allows us to sleep, and enables us to rise in the morning feeling good about the day. This is the wisdom behind the biblical admonition to not let the sun go down on unresolved irritations, annoyances, and hurts. "Do not let the sun go down on your anger" (Eph. 4:26). As couples we need to seek this closure to the day because of its value to ourselves and our marriage. The need to appease our partner or to appease our own conscience may start us in the right direction, but the best motivation is adult wisdom.

The rewards of a good closure to the day make it worth the effort. It is good preparation for an evening devotional time together. When the obstacles have been cleared by the dialogue of sharing and reconciliation, each can participate genuinely in prayer together, being open with God and with the other. It is also good preparation for sexual intimacy. If couples enter into sexual intimacy when they are not intimate in spirit, there is a built-in obstacle to full participation. This is particularly true for the woman, who is less likely to use sex for verbalizing and reconciliation than is the man.

Becoming reconciled—making up—is itself an act of closeness that creates warmth. When this marvelous experience occurs, the partners may desire to express this closeness holistically—to express it sexually. They want to get "real close" to make up for the separation. The contrast between the way they feel after being reconciled and the alienation they felt prior to this leads them to want to celebrate. George Bach is so sold on this connection that he offers the slogan "Love, Fight and Grow!"[11]

When reconciliation takes place, we are accepted by each other in our vulnerability so that we can drop our defenses and begin to experience humility. Then we can "see" the real person communicating through the body, and we want to reach out to this person and embrace the body that communicates it. Reconciliation, thus, in itself is a stimulus for sexual intimacy.

Regressions are hard to take since they seem to disavow the progress we thought we were making. Betty and Matt had this experience during a party which should have been a time of gaiety. In the early years of their marriage Matt had the tendency to forget about Betty at parties and become totally engrossed with others—often other women. They had reached an understanding after many unhappy aftermaths, and Matt had been sensitive to Betty's needs at social gatherings for some time. But then it happened: he became engrossed again with a small group of people at a party who shared many of his political concerns. He literally forgot Betty was even present. The experience took Betty back to those earlier years as though there had been none intervening, as if they were only pretense and illusion. For Matt it was simply a time when he became careless. He thought he had it made—that it would not happen again—and losing awareness of his vulnerability, he was drawn into the stimulating conversation to the extent that he

Through Forgiveness to Intimacy

became oblivious not only to Betty but to the passage of time. For Betty, reconciliation seemed to be out of the question. Instead she despaired over her marriage.

Does forgiveness still apply to Betty and Matt? In this relapse has it lost its meaning and effectiveness? When does it no longer apply? Jesus was asked this question. "Lord, how often shall my brother sin against me, and I forgive him? As many as seven times?" Jesus replied, "I do not say to you seven times, but seventy times seven" (Matt. 18:21-22). In saying this Jesus was reversing the usual understanding of reconciliation. Rather than thinking of it as a limited privilege, he saw it as a continuous way of showing care. What regressions require, therefore, is another application of forgiveness. Everything changes to the positive when we allow God's forgiveness to be reapplied to our marital union—even in our experience of regression. When we let ourselves give and receive forgiveness once more, grace truly abounds.

An essential part of this abounding grace is that God can use our marital conflicts—even our marital regressions—to bring us closer together. The renewed application of the cure can increase our realization of intimacy, and in so doing is an assist in the process of becoming one flesh—of practicing marriage. There is a wealth of insight available through reconciliation since we can look without repulsion at what was going on. These insights can become helpful knowledge for future experiences. The lowering of our defenses which takes place in reconciliation helps us to see not only our behavior but also the motivations behind it.

Marge was deeply troubled by the repeated hassles between her and Wayne. She knew that they had come from homes of different emotional climates, but she could not understand the apparent stalemate in adjusting. In their marriage enrichment group, as they talked about their latest conflict, she saw for the first time the reaction pattern that she had brought into her marriage. Whenever she was yelled at—and Wayne could yell—she deteriorated emotionally on the spot. She became like a panicky child and wept uncontrollably in her agony. Could she become free of this reaction? The achievement of this insight in itself gave her hope. If her reaction had been conditioned *in*, could it not—with the help of her group and Wayne—be conditioned *out*? She could entertain that goal only if she could *live* with regressions.

Wayne on the other hand had also needed insight into *himself* at these times. At first he would defend himself against the severity of Marge's reaction. He began what he thought was a reasonable approach with the words, "All I said was . . ." But his defense was not reasonable to Marge. The group encouraged him to take a deeper look—to relive the most recent "bad scene" and ask not only what he said, but how he said it: the tone of his voice, the volume, the nonverbal facial expression.

Wayne and Marge's situation shows why marital partners need to withhold their judgment of the other in their conflicts. *Both* are in need of understanding—of forgiveness. Both are coping not just with this moment, but with their whole personal development—the baggage that they brought into their relationship. This is not to justify any bad actions. There are times when one partner is obviously "out of line"— when the behavior is grievously offensive. Yet partners can deal more constructively with this behavior when both are aware that they have received forgiveness from God.

Forgiveness makes growth possible. This is true both for personal growth and for the growth of our marriage relationship. Forgiveness ends the destructive role of guilt. Until it is resolved in reconciliation, our guilt predisposes us to repeat rather than to cease the behavior over which we feel guilty. Forgiveness, as we have seen, allows the past to be *past*. We often find it hard to let go of the past, even though we could be free of it. We need to let the old pass away—to let the new begin—to let forgiveness suffice for the past. Insight into our behavior and that of our mate never comes too late if there is still time to do things differently. Faith in God—trust in God's providence— replaces the need to change the past with a hopeful vision of the future. Within the covenant of forgiveness we can let go of the past and allow ourselves a genuinely fresh start.

3

Sex Role Conflicts

Going into any novelty shop reaffirms how little actual change the sexual revolution has made. "Men work from dawn to dusk, but women's work is never done" still sells well. The battle of the sexes is possibly as old as humankind. Marriage is the prime stage for the continuing drama. We ourselves did not escape it. The unevenness of sharing responsibilities for joint tenancy, especially if there are children, weighs heavily upon the woman. Sometimes we blame the Judeo-Christian heritage for our problem. Any cursory reading of the literature of the American Indian or African will undo this idea.

THE THWARTING OF WOMEN'S GROWTH

Looking at our Scriptures, however, does cause confusion. Proverbs 31:10-31, so often cited as a proof of a woman's worth, shows us a woman with a dizzying schedule, completely selfless. "She puts her hands to the distaff, and her hands hold the spindle. She opens her hand to the poor, and reaches out her hands to the needy. . . . She looks well to the ways of her household, and does not eat the bread of idleness." Orthodox Jewish men still sing this to their wives every Sabbath.[1] Women of today identify well with the woman of Proverbs as she juggles career, family, and marriage. Unfortunately, the ritual of special affirmation is omitted from Christian practices.

In Judy Syfers's well-known essay, "I Want a Wife,"[2] Syfers puts in her request for the same services men expect and ends with "My God, who wouldn't want a wife?" In sharp satire, Syfers describes a wife as one who takes care of her husband. His physical needs are her priority. She will keep the house clean remembering that it is for him. He will not need to pick up after himself. She will keep a running inventory of repaired, clean, ready-to-wear clothing. Replacing any garments as needed is part of that service. Her filing system will be so ingenious that her husband can find any necessary item immediately.

In the years since the essay was written, Lucy has used it in many class discussions. Men, more and more, see Syfers's view as outdated. Some are already contributing the services mentioned. One wrote, "I want a husband, one who will keep a job, fix the plumbing, change the oil in the car, and meet emergency needs for big muscles."[3]

Women of all generations have had to deal with the restraints of sex roles. Women who were permitted an education were exceptions, most often their lives were not in service to males. Without an education, without a wide perspective, women would not have been able to conceive of other than the traditional way of living.

A secure male, like the husband of Proverbs must have been, will encourage a woman to reach fulfillment; an insecure one will try to control the woman. It is sometimes argued that education is wasted on women. Marriage and family counselor Evelyn Millis Duvall had a mother who believed in education for women. Her father did not. Duvall was educated against her father's wishes. "She'll only get married," he said.[4]

Devotion to the homemaking arts as the arena for women in the fifties set the stage for the feminist movement in the seventies. As a person who was educated during World War II, Lucy participated in this overemphasis. Many of our industries made their start in this period. New machinery was invented and manufactured intended for women whose chief concern would be homemaking. The current trend toward shared homemaking has altered this market only slightly. Magazines for the homemaker, with advice on economy, entertaining, and bedroom conduct, flourished heavily during the fifties to seventies era. Subtly or not so subtly their message was that with the proper conduct of the wife in the home, the husband would be motivated to succeed.[5]

The appeal depended strongly upon the insecurity of the woman. The postwar boom raised living standards. Conduct and values learned under modest circumstances would not do for affluent circumstances.

Sex Role Conflicts

In effect, how-to-do-it magazines and books replaced the authority of the older generation. Childbirth in hospitals, bottle feeding, and suburban living had not been the previous generation's experience. It seemed that printed material was the only place to look for answers. Magazines today have adapted their material in much the same way to the upwardly mobile "yuppies," telling them how to cope with two careers, family, and marriage. Managing household help is a big topic today as nannies and housekeepers have returned to middle-class homes.

The role of women has changed in recent decades. Soldiers who returned from Vietnam did not find women leaving the workplace as they did after previous wars. Women have become a permanent part of the American workplace. Company wives, totally devoted to the husband's success, are nearly gone.

Sex roles play into the manipulative pressure of advertisement. Since women still perform most of the household tasks in addition to parenting and business responsibilities, they are still the chief consumer for the household. They no longer produce directly the articles which clothe and feed the family; now women are urged to "buy this and try that." Whereas soap, ammonia, and vinegar cleaned most household items for many years, today one of woman's functions in keeping clothes clean and food cooked means being able to *choose* between many similar products. Her family is now taken care of by a myriad of medical developments. Products and medical care have helped the woman move beyond the home in a way her great-grandparents would have seen as scandalous. Whereas the mothers and grandmothers of former generations would have been confined to the house for weeks when childhood diseases struck, today's mother will fear only a few health problems.

Even so, family roles still have to be negotiated. When a child is sick, we are not yet accustomed to the man being absent from work. Perhaps some men have become accustomed to sharing child care with a wife whose job responsibilities are as financially important as his. The woman who, in former generations, resented being so very tied to the home, now has choices which heretofore were not even envisioned. She is in essence the nurturing parent but with a new twist. Because she is no longer financially powerless, she has added responsibilities for the home. Coping with these additional responsibilities will mean defining a new role.

The clash of past and present roles has created dilemmas for the family. The effect of women being limited to the home and to being the "woman behind the man" had its drawbacks. Lacking power in any other sphere, the woman exercised too much power in the home, power which she really did not want! Formerly we accepted that a man had to neglect his home to succeed in the marketplace. Today it seems that both women and men have to neglect the home to succeed.[6]

Because of these pressures, men may be confused about their role in the home. Children neglected by the confused father become, then, the center of a woman's life. Not many fathers even in today's liberated home would be able to say what Evelyn Millis Duvall's husband said when a neighbor asked who was going to keep the children while the mother was on a trip, "Fortunately our children have *two* parents."[7] Until recently it was certainly a rare man who could adjust to his wife having a place in "a man's world," and would share in the homemaking and child rearing.

On top of all that, the household-magazine advice was that women learn to "talk" to a man, which really meant listening to him. Few husbands gave credit to their wives' contribution to their careers. The former Mrs. Benjamin Spock was very angry at the time of her divorce because she was left without credit for her research contributions to her husband's work. Who has not known women who have asked their husbands to present ideas in groups because the idea would be heard more favorably "coming from a man"?

In practicing marriage, husbands and wives will not sidestep gender conflict, but will learn to forgive each other and acquire a new perspective about who they really are. Insights from psychology and theology can help them take stock of where they have been and where they are going. They can learn to appreciate the many possibilities in this time of change as challenges rather than as burdens. Life no longer needs to be a headlong race for success. Life can be filled with an appreciation of what they have learned and with a sense of adventure about what they can yet learn and do. Rifts that have been caused by set ideas about sex roles can now be reevaluated. Dan Kiley, to whom we referred previously, says that even Peter Pans can change. A woman who recognizes she is in a dead-end relationship with such a man should get her own house in order.[8] If just one partner makes a goal of finding satisfying sex roles, progress in the marriage will more likely happen.

ADAPTABILITY AT ANY AGE

As literary critics have observed, rites of passage, in literature as in life, reflect the prevailing values of culture. This is especially true of the passage between childhood and adulthood. Gail Sheehy's book *Passages* has helped us to realize that there are more passages in life than that of child to adult. Yet Sheehy's book stops at middle age. Someone needs to write the book that covers the subject from that point on. Marriage is a lifelong process, and guidance for sex role adjustments following midlife are either vague or unwritten.

There have been times when we have been disappointed, each with the other. Most married people have had similar experiences. Instead of being shocked and fantasizing a quick escape from the problem, we ought to pause to understand what caused the problem (much as one runs through a mental checklist when an appliance malfunctions). Marriage could then become the place for maturing it was meant to be. Conflict over sex roles would probably head the checklist.

As we mature, the power to apply knowledge and wisdom comes to us; it takes an act of the will to resist the knee-jerk responses of our "child." Our will must challenge the thought that "she (or he) will never change." "Too late" are the devil's own words. After middle age those words can become a shout if we let them. If, however, we believe that change is always possible, middle age and beyond has its own passages into new stages of life. This means that women and men can learn to take new roles. This belief opens up workable alternatives to giving up on a marriage in order to get a new start in life. Women have learned to maintain cars and men have learned to nurture children. Traditional roles can be challenged at any age.

Whatever changes are needed to make the partnership work are predicated on the assumption that each partner has the self-esteem to be aware of personal needs. We have to learn to nurture others and become our own nurturer as well. Self-responsibility means taking positive steps for our own well-being.

The change of traditional roles can be unsettling. When a husband sees his wife coping well with complicated financial transactions, when a woman sees a husband who was "never good with children" being obviously adored by grandchildren, they may feel threatened. One's identity beyond familiar roles must be nurtured. Then we can discover in our adulthood our own roles and learn to function in any task.

CHANGES CAN LEAD TO PATIENCE AND COMPASSION

The changes in our culture regarding sex roles are potentially good for marriage. Adjustment in marriage before these changes came about was too easy—societal expectations for the sexes, particularly in marriage, left many possibilities and, therefore, opportunities, closed off. Male and female roles and needs were clearly labeled: "Men are like this, women like that; men need this, women that." Such labels are generalizations which spare us the effort of thinking: they characterize a lazy mind.

When we were a young family, a respected man in our community used these labels to such an extent that his sense of responsibility blocked his sensitivity and even his generosity. His wife wanted to get a job. They had no children, and both were middle-aged. In John's mind, a man who did not support his wife was no man! John had his own business and was doing well; so obviously she did not need the money. John gave her an ultimatum: if she got a job, he would sell his business and go fishing. He meant it. A major reason for John's working was to support his wife. It was his way of caring for her, of loving her. The community knew of his stance and respected him for it. He was not only a "real man," but a responsible husband. Yet it was really a sad decision because in the name of love he blocked his wife from developing her life as she desired. It was not money she needed. What she needed was a challenge—an outlet for her energies.

Because of the greater emancipation from sex roles in the present, we are free to go beyond the cultural stereotypes to understand the needs of each partner. Because of stereotypes, women have been forced into manipulative ways of gaining status within marriage. As a child Bill remembers seeing a wall hanging of a poem, the gist of which was that a clever wife let her husband think he was the boss so that she could have her way. We laughed at that sort of thing then—men did too. After all, it allowed the men to keep their authority in the home—at least in the abstract, since the roles were still intact.

The habits and behavior patterns developed then are still with us. A woman whose husband shares equally the housework and the parenting showed us that she still operated in manipulative terms when she said, "Men are like race horses. Keep them well fed, throw a warm blanket over them at night, keep them happy—and you can get them to do anything you want."

The key to genuine emancipation from sex roles within marriage is to establish a climate in which each partner regards and values the other as a distinct and unique individual. Each is a partner together in a one-flesh relationship. This kind of climate allows each to discover the other, to plumb the unlimited dimensions of the other's person. The emancipation from sex roles in marriage creates a more demanding but also a more fulfilling climate for marriage. It creates the conditions that enable the partners to develop within a wide range of possibilities, so that talents may not remain hidden.

Because of our fixed images of how things should be, we all find it difficult to change our ways. And it is truly difficult! Yet as we make the effort to free ourselves from old sex roles, we will become more free to make creative decisions in our marriage. This in itself is enriching for marriage since decision making by consensus is a good relational exercise.

Sexism presents all sorts of obstacles to becoming one flesh, because its many forms are damaging to the development of the individual—whether male or female. Although composer Gustav Mahler married a very talented musician, he insisted that her career must end with the marriage so that she could assist him in furthering his own career. His society, of course, supported him in this unilateral decision. After all, he was not only a man, he was the *husband*. As late as the 1950s we were still saying, "Behind every successful man is a supportive woman."

Yet what the people of Mahler's day and even of the postwar period did not realize was that when a woman is held back to further a man, the man also is held back—not necessarily professionally, but as a person. While we were in England on a sabbatical in the late fifties, for example, our neighbors shared with us that they were watching Bill to see if he helped with the dishes or other cleaning. American men were supposedly more domesticated than the English men. Since he had occasionally helped with the dishes, he had mixed feelings about their conclusion. He remembers that he did not want them to view him as something less than a man, while at the same time it felt good (now and then) to step out of the prescribed role to "help out." Naturally, he expected appreciation! Bill now realizes that he continued to assume that his work was the more important. Being clergy reinforced this attitude since clergy responsibilities, then confined to men, were obviously given priority.

When as peers in a marriage we have to consider another's interests without the easy route of fixed images of male and female responsibilities, we are encouraged to grow in patience and compassion. Though we cannot make our decisions as quickly as when we depended on fixed roles, we can make *better* decisions and make them in better ways. When we allow ourselves to listen, we open ourselves to compassion.

Compassion is a male as well as female attribute. When men can accept their compassionate nature they are affirming their maleness. The qualities associated with the male stereotype give a false picture of masculinity. In the portrayal of God in the Bible the writers use the male pronoun and the father role because they were the only ones available or acceptable to the mind-set of the day. Yet when these same writers describe the *qualities* of God, the concept of maleness loses its cultural significance. God is a father who is compassionate toward God's children (Ps. 103:13). Though a man, Jesus described his feelings toward the people of Jerusalem as those of a hen that desires to gather her chicks under her wings in motherly affection and protection (Matt. 23:27).

The end of sex role assumptions opens the door to individual and mutual opportunities which will increase rather than decrease conflict. Vivian and Phil are examples of these new choices. Vivian is an accomplished painter. Phil is a rising young business executive. Vivian wants to establish herself as an artist, which means living in a community with opportunities for doing this. Phil wants to advance in the company and to do this he may have to accept a series of transfers. How will they work out a decision if either has an opportunity to move where the other will have less opportunity? Both believe in the calling of God in their lives and both are committed to a peer relationship in their marriage. They know they may have to endure much pain in making future decisions.

Freedom from gender roles does not take away a woman's option to give her full time to homemaking. If it did we would only be creating new fixed images in place of previous ones. Women who desire to do so, however, may feel less than adequate in our day. Finances are a major consideration. Barbara is an example. Although she has a skill that is valued in the business world and has worked to support her family while her husband attended college, she now wishes to stay home with their children. Her husband realizes it will be tough getting along on his beginning salary, but he respects Barbara's desire. Because they arrived at their decision by consensus, they both desire to make it work. Other couples have decided to share equally in the responsibilities for breadwinning and child caring. To assure the children of adequate parenting, they may arrange for each to work part time during these years.

FACING CONFLICTS OPENLY

It is easy to become resigned to a "that's the way it is" marriage. Shutting down one's feelings is a temptation. Neither of us was ready to do this. The area of gender roles was a field of conflict for us. Many questions arose in the day-to-day working out of particulars so that the house, children, and work could run smoothly. They still do not. Now that we are near retiring and want to continue to do well in our vocations, neither of us wants to take out the garbage. There are real questions concerning which of us does which task and whether this is mutually agreeable or assumed. Our friends who are retired also face this dilemma. The best thing we have going for us is our communication, even at increased decibels if necessary. The spiritual growth which we believe attends our struggles is not what we had thought spiritual growth was about when we married.

As poet Gerhard Frost says, "Never kill a question!"[9] The words imply that questions are alive, and they are. Struggling with them brings growth. When we answer the questions that arise—"What is happening? and How do I feel about it?"—we are asking *observing* questions. When we ask "What does my ethical system and faith in God say about both of those questions?" we have moved to a deeper love. Now we can begin to understand true freedom. We can know ourselves and others and make real choices, rather than being predisposed by forces we do not understand.

Today's couples may be feeling the effect of a previous generation of women who have repressed their conflict over sex roles. Such women were very controlling and at the same time sad in spirit. They may unthinkingly project their conflicts onto the next generation. A woman whom we met at a marriage workshop could not keep her mind on the workshop exercises. She was bothered by questions about equality in marriage. Her thinking was colored by her mother-in-law's insistence that her life had been exemplary because she had not worked outside the home, and her children had always been considered first. When this woman wanted to be employed, her mother-in-law was obviously threatened. The leaving of father and mother was difficult for the wife and the husband in this situation even though both were highly educated. It will take a great deal of love and patience on the part of all three in this drama to become free and loving.

Her mother-in-law's sacrifice had a controlling influence upon her family. They were made to feel that considering anything "less" for their lives than a home in which there was a full-time homemaking mother, no matter what the circumstances, was disloyal to her. While genuine sacrifice is noble, one that is used to control others is crippling. There is not much growth where all the conditions are preordained. Excitement, however, can be shared by all members of a family working creatively toward their goals. Both women and men can experience what psychologist Wayne Dyer noted of his mother, "She did not complain because there was hope rather than resignation."[10] Her sacrifice had validity. Young husbands and wives, however, are very vulnerable to coercion by their parents, and in such instances the children may have to discipline the parents. Each person in a family unit needs to choose his or her options. How wonderful it is to have the support of a mate and not an obvious sacrifice.

One of our big mistakes as a new couple was in seeing the ideal home as a place without argument and conflict. They were negative factors. Therefore, in our eyes, conflict had to be a secret and usually produced bad feelings. Good Christians we believed were irenic, smiling, and at ease. Conflict distorted such pictures, and so we always obscured the negative. We wanted to look well. At the same time we wanted our life to be authentic.

We perceive this is also the experience of other couples. When we marry we expect to be where others are after a lifetime of growing.

The promises of God depend on our coming to grips with our conflicts and other growth challenges. Saint Paul said to put on the whole armor of God. It would take the whole armor of God to deal with repressed anger over which one is ashamed.

As a couple we came to realize how far different our images of home really were. Since we shared a religious and ethical viewpoint, the other points for quarreling could be addressed and we did not withdraw. That meant that we had conflict and we had to deal with it. Lucy came from a farm background, Bill a city. Lucy's people were American for many generations whereas Bill's grandparents came here as adults. Lucy's family is large, Bill's is small. We both had assimilated very definite ideas about daily living patterns and the picture of home. Becoming a unit of our own involved a continuous process in which each had to be aware of the other and the other's needs. That was not and is not easy.

A way in which couples can discover some of the obstacles that are preventing them from growing as a couple is for each to prepare a list of the positive and negative influences and views of sex roles of their own families of origin. After preparing their lists each shares and discusses it with the other. This is a time for listening to the other and not for correcting or advising. The advantage of this exercise is that it opens each partner's eyes to the other's awareness of these influences.

BACKUP IN OUR MARRIAGE WITH CHRIST

As we have seen, the changes that have taken place in the roles of husband and wife contain the potential for increased conflict in marriage. Most of us view conflict as damaging to marriage, and so changes that create conflict are deemed bad for marriage. This is unfortunate not only because it is an erroneous understanding of conflict but also because our view of conflict affects our behavior in conflict. We need to view conflict positively because it *is* potentially positive. Once we believe this we will behave differently when faced with conflict. Conflict management specialist G. Douglas Lewis views conflict as an "intervention of the Holy Spirit that opens up new possibilities for both parties to grow and change."[11]

Most of us tend to avoid conflict as much as we can in the hope that it will go away. It rarely does. Instead it may grow worse since suppressed irritations lead us to distance ourselves emotionally from those who irritate us. On the other hand, when we view conflict positively, we are likely to deal directly with it. When we do, we are just as likely to discover that the experience will lead us into greater intimacy.

Sex role conflicts are positive for marriage because they provide more opportunity for developing the one-flesh relationship. The increased conflict due to these changes comes from the expansion of choices for each partner. As we deal with these conflicts together as couples, our experience of *being married* is expanded.

Some have seen these sex role changes as disruptive to marriage. There is the familiar story of the disenchanted wife, who, believing she has missed out on much in life by being confined to family responsibilities, wants her freedom, not only from the marriage but sometimes also from the care and custody of children. The women's liberation movement has taken the rap for such marital disruptions. It is charged with creating discontent with the traditional roles of wife and mother. We humans, it is true, are readily susceptible to those who wish to make us dissatisfied. The very fact that others are getting more than I am is enough for me to become discontented with my lot—even if I was contented before becoming aware of the discrepancy. If we add to this human penchant for envy the influence of the human potential movement and its emphasis on seeking one's own fulfillment, we have all the cultural conditioning necessary for chafing under any obligations that seem to hold us down. Men have also been known to walk out on their marital and parental responsibilities long before our modern era. The only difference now is that women are accused of doing the same thing.

Men also are affected by sex role changes. The previously fixed roles protected the male's control. Now with the liberation of women from these roles, some males have felt that they were losing control—whether in the home or in the marketplace. This can be frightening. If one is used to the dominant role one finds it difficult to give up this power, and to have peer relationships in the home and in the marketplace.

Some have "wanted out" of their marriage because of this increased conflict. Their negative view of conflict has lowered their tolerance for it, and they want to end what seems to be meaningless pain. Marriage and divorce counselor Mel Krantzler, who wrote *Creative Divorce* after his divorce, now has written *Creative Marriage* after his second marriage. In this book he acknowledges that he has changed his mind regarding the potentials of the marriage relationship. "There is more gold to be mined in your relationship with your spouse than you may suspect," he writes. Krantzler entered into his first marriage believing that a good marriage was a problem-free marriage. But he learned that the best of marriages are subject to many problems. His marriage, in contrast to his ideal, seemed to be a breeding ground for problems, and he "wallowed in the belief that the grass was greener in other couple's gardens." Now he has reversed himself. "The grass can be greener," he says, "inside your marriage rather than outside it."[12]

Sex Role Conflicts

The negative aspect of conflict is not in conflict itself but in its mismanagement. Instead of utilizing it to deepen the relationship, we allow it instead to stifle it.

We have a resource for dealing with conflict in our marriage with Christ. While this marriage does not automatically provide the wisdom to manage conflict well, it does provide us with the inner security to accept change—even in our gender roles. Though these may change, our bond with Christ remains, providing meaning in the midst of change. Transitional times like ours are threatening to meaning. We have put our faith in *forms*—which are by their very nature changeable—instead of in the truths expressed through the forms. But when our faith is in God rather than in the forms, we have the stability we need to hang on through the growing pains of marital conflict. Because of our faith we can view these conflicts as processes in God's providence. Consequently, we do not limit God's options to those perceived by our limited vision. Instead we see through the "eyes of faith." This enables us to trust that there is meaning in our struggles even when we are engaged in conflict.

Our marriage with Christ gives us our identity. It is this identity that we bring to our marriage and to its conflicts. Our marriage with Christ contains our calling—our vocation. As covenanted people we are called to live for more than our own interest and comforts. We are called to love even when love leads us into the discomforts of conflict.

How can love lead us into conflict? When we care about our mate and our marriage we stimulate and challenge them both. If we back away from the conflicts that such challenging may produce, we are caring more about our own distaste for conflict than about our mate and our marriage.

LIBERATION AS PERSONS

The liberation of women from stereotyped roles both as women and as wives has been long overdue. As this liberation is taking hold in our society it will indeed create conflict in marriages. The challenge to the partners is not to run from these tensions, but to work on managing them for the growth of the relationship. Men also are in need of liberation, both as men and as husbands. It is impossible for one sex to be liberated without liberating the other. When the system is altered by one of its parts, the other parts also must change. Men are already experiencing this liberation, in their growing awareness that expressing their tender feelings, their fears, their weaknesses is no threat to their masculinity.

But liberation as men and as women, though greatly needed from our repressive gender stereotypes, does not go far enough in affecting change. What is needed is a more basic liberation as *persons*. Our person is prior to our gender. If we are not liberated in our persons, gender liberation may fail to be genuinely liberating.

Without the liberation of our persons other liberations may take on the character of emulating those who formerly were "on top." Equality then means becoming like those whose position in society we had formerly envied. As the Danish philosopher Soren Kierkegaard observed, "Envy is secret admiration."[13] Without a sense of our own identity as persons we may take on the characteristics—even the undesirable characteristics—of our former oppressors.

There is evidence that this is already happening in the liberation of women. A study of five hundred career men and women revealed that women suffer the same stress-related health problems as men when they take on the "macho" qualities of concealing their feelings and being preoccupied with work and success.[14]

There is little one can do about the external stresses—often due to conflicts—in the competitive milieu of our marketplace. There is much that we can do about our *internal* stress—our response to these external stresses. The ability to cope with external stress comes from knowing who we are as persons, and specifically, knowing who we are in relationship to God. A practical effect of believing in God is believing also in ourselves as men or women. We carry within us the qualities of community, of trust, of faith because we are bonded to Christ. Our faith in ourselves is based on our identity under God. There is no hierarchy, gender or otherwise, in God's community. We are equal as persons and divine grace is the equalizer. "For as many of you as were baptized into Christ have put on Christ. There is neither slave nor free, there is neither male or female, for you are all one in Christ Jesus" (Gal. 3:27-28). Women always were equal with men in God's eyes. No cultural stereotypes should be permitted to make it otherwise.

If both partners know the satisfaction of growth as persons, it is easier to live with the choices they make as peers in the marriage. They are made in the trust that they are the best choices for them as a couple in the process of their mutual development.

4
Prosperity and Adversity

In the vows that we took when we were married we promised to love each other "in prosperity and adversity." Now, one version of the marriage service reads "share all that is to come," and "your joys and sorrows." In our view the older version said a lot more. Prosperity comes from two Latin words meaning "answering to hope" or "the realization of one's hopes." Adversity comes from two Latin words meaning "turning to" or "opposing," therefore, "opposition to one's hopes." Prosperity means good fortune or good luck; adversity, bad fortune or bad luck. The words, thus, were an explanation of the vow to love unconditionally. It is this love that is the bonding agent in marriage; it holds in prosperity and in adversity. "Joys and sorrows" is not an adequate substitute. While prosperity may bring a transitory happiness, it may not bring joy. Sorrow, while closer to adversity, lacks the objective tone of the latter.

IN PROSPERITY

Obviously we prefer prosperity to adversity. Why not? Who would not want to prosper—have good fortune—have one's hopes fulfilled? Yet there is no evidence that prosperity is helpful to a marriage. In fact it has often been recognized as a disintegrating influence in marriage. "The worst thing that can happen to one is that one gets everything that one desires." Why is such good luck considered a bad omen? It is because prosperity has a way of corrupting us.

Take economic prosperity, for example. A common observation is

51

that it can "turn one's head"—that is, it can make one feel superior. Prosperity can entice us away from our center, our source—from God—to becoming our *own* center. We are then off-centered according to the way God created us; so we cast a shadow. This shadow often falls on the marital relationship. Instead of moving us to gratitude, our prosperity can move us to greed for more. As William Sloane Coffin says, "There are two ways to be rich. One is to have lots of money, the other to have few needs."[1] The latter is the one emphasized in our biblical heritage since "spiritual resources are likely to be more available when our economic resources are not in excess."[2]

What is said about economic prosperity can be said about other kinds of prosperity as well. Those who have never failed in an endeavor or never had a serious illness may be unprepared not only for future adversity but also to feel with those who are experiencing failure or illness. They may even believe that they are healthy and prosperous because of their own efforts.

Perhaps the designers of these old vows did not intend prosperity and adversity as good and bad opposites for marriage, but rather as two kinds of hazards for marriage. As the proverb says, "Give me neither poverty nor riches" (Prov. 30:18). Saint Paul thought it a mark of spiritual maturity that he "knew the secret of plenty and hunger, abundance and want" (Phil. 4:12). Material scarcity puts a strain on marriage but so does material prosperity. There are familiar stories of marital stress due to both. Scarcity creates frustrations that are often projected onto the partner, while prosperity entices us into the value and priority system of our culture in which "more" is better.

The very means for becoming and remaining prosperous are frequently obstacles to marital growth. One such obstacle is the "career first" priority in which marriage and family and even the larger community are all neglected. A means for becoming and remaining prosperous is a frequent obstacle to marital growth, namely, the addiction to work which often characterizes successful people in our culture. In this addiction, values relating to marriage and family are sacrificed. If this is the price for success, it is too high. Even if we do succeed, the problems only worsen. Our increasing possessions have a way of increasingly possessing *us*. They take time and energy to manage and maintain. Our schedule becomes a master to which we increasingly lose our freedom.

In addition, our acquisitions require locks and fences—symbols of our loss of community. Meanwhile our acquisitiveness continues unabated. Few among us can say "enough is enough" once we get involved in the prosperity syndrome. We no longer travel lightly through our earthly pilgrimage. Instead our involvement in our culture's values becomes a heavy weight of stress. The imbalance of life style that results tends to starve our relationships. Marriage can be the first casualty of this imbalance.

IN ADVERSITY

All people fear adversity—and rightly so. Adversities can be devastating. When we think of adversity in our own marriage, we immediately think of our *big* adversity. We had had our ups and downs in our life together. But when we experienced the loss of our oldest daughter in a tragic death, all of our other adversities seemed to pale. We had no real warning. Our daughter was married and lived several hundred miles away. The suddenness of the death was obviously a great shock, but the shock did not numb our pain, which seemed intolerable. We seriously wondered how or even if we would survive. One of the most comforting expressions of sympathy was the word of a colleague who said, "If this were to happen to me, I honestly don't know whether I could take it." We knew he *understood*.

As we stood at the graveside of our daughter we were living a moment we had not anticipated. It just did not happen to parents in our generation; rather it was children who stood at the graveside of their parents. Yet the parents of previous generations faced this experience often, as do parents in today's underdeveloped countries. Because we have pushed back the time of dying in our culture, we can be under the illusion that death is an abstraction, reserved for a long time ahead. The death rate, however, remains what it has always been—100 percent. Nor was the loss of a child probably any less devastating to the parents of former years when it occurred more frequently, or any less devastating to the parents of today's young black males whose rate of death by homicide is phenomenally high.

The adversity of loss—like the prosperity of success—can prove too much for the marriage. In a research study conducted by the University of Minnesota with the families of fifty-seven children who had died following terminal illnesses, this strain on the marriage was evident.

"The divorce rate among such families tends to be high." Women particularly talked about the difficulty they had in "maintaining equilibrium in their marriage" following their child's death. "I don't know what happened," one mother said. "All of a sudden we were at each other's throats all the time." Another said, "My husband won't talk about Cindy. I want to. I *have* to talk about her, but he never says a word. We don't communicate at all anymore."[3]

In such an adversity one spouse may blame the other—usually for some inadequacy in parenting. Sometimes this is a legitimate complaint, or a problem long before the child's death, but now resentment comes out in full force. Parents, like others, feel the need for a scapegoat in these adversities and the mate is convenient for this purpose. Blaming the other may be one's way of staying a step ahead of despairing, but the marriage bond weakens under the pressure. For in blaming the mate one is cutting off one's major source of support for restoration to life—for survival. We say that time heals such wounds, but this is not so. Time helps—but healing also requires healthy grieving. For such grieving we need intimate sharing relationships—and one's mate is a natural for this purpose because he or she shares the same pain.

Several years following our daughter's death a friend brought a woman, whose son had died tragically, to our house so that we might talk with her. We asked about her husband, since he also had suffered the same loss. "We haven't a good relationship," she said. "He blames me because I went to work while our son was growing up." How sad! They both need each other and yet are perpetuating an old estrangement. What she and others in similar adversity need is to be reconciled with their mates so that their one-flesh relationship can sustain them both in their pain.

THE POSITIVE SIDE

Tragedy or adversity can also draw couples closer together. This may run counter to statistics, but one can see why this possibility must be taken seriously. Most of our philosophy and culture teaches us not to accept imperfection, and tragedy and adversity are always running counter to what is supposed to be! They are inconveniences. We plan and expect our lives to unfold in an orderly way, where the unexpected does not occur. When events go counter to plans, we and others cannot wait for things to "return to normal." We naturally want things as

Prosperity and Adversity

they were. In struggling through the adversity to which we have referred, we knew intimately how the temptation to go separate ways comes to a couple.

In these new circumstances, old friends may fade away. The support that we expect comes, but often from unexpected sources. Those we had our fun with find it hard to fit in with us now. They were our good-time buddies. When one loses a child, other families may shy away from the bereaved; the thought that it could happen to them is too frightening to consider.

What can draw a couple together is the very uniqueness of their experience. No one else knows us as does our mate; no one else knows the secret failings and surprising triumphs. Even so, we know from our own experience that in the face of adversity it often takes an act of the will to work together. How easy it is to write these words and how hard to do them! The tension of facing the problem itself and the added dimension of purposefully working as a team was very present in our tragedy. We could have allowed a second tragedy.

At the time of adversity a searching of one's own personality is often in order. Lucy acknowledges a tendency to go it alone. Bill tends to retreat or lean upon others. While it is not exactly what one wants to think about at this time, and may be difficult to face, if a couple is not to pull apart, they need to give attention to these personality tendencies. We are not amazed that marriages break up in the face of crises. We know the temptation to walk away and not deal with the crisis or to go one's separate way, guessing and half understanding our spouse's pain. As we know from experience, it is best to feel the whole of the pain and deal with the other partner sensitively in order to overcome the tendency to evade. A high level of trust develops when two people express their feelings and deal with everything that comes up. Unless the couple intentionally works this through together, the feeling of loneliness in the presence of the only one who could possibly understand becomes a deep-seated disappointment.

Resignation is the worst thing that can happen at a crisis time. One may be resigned to the conclusion that the mate cannot be counted on. A person who regularly faces life's challenges with resignation needs help. If this is your tendency, perhaps you can attack it on other levels where there is no crisis.

Marriage is for the growth of both partners. In adversity each will need to talk it out with the other and each will need to share the intimacy of suffering. Fear that the marriage may look bad, that one cannot cope, is often more of a problem than the crisis itself. Rarely do we know ourselves well enough to predict when our shadow side or subconscious will bubble up. In any crisis the mind may suddenly flood with thoughts, pictures, and feelings which one had long forgotten or thought of no significance. Old wounds may open again when this is done. This can be confusing to both partners, especially if the content seems irrational. Panic often sets in at adversity. The reactions can take either partner by surprise.

When families live far from the homes of origin during bereavement, the only person with whom to share is the mate. When Lucy's father died, she was not ready for general expressions of sympathy. She was glad the others expressed sympathy, but actually Bill was the only one who knew anything of her relationship to her father.

The willingness to accept and acknowledge genuine failure takes a mature person. It also takes practice. The confession "I was wrong," for many of us, is hard to get our mouths around. And sometimes the bigger the failing the harder it is to admit it. As mentioned previously, this is especially true when the partner might later misuse the information to retaliate and wound the other. The Finns have a word for the quality of character that is needed at this time. They call it *sitsu*. It combines the qualities of vulnerability and toughness. The transparency of self which allows one the freedom to admit failure or fault without allowing others to victimize is very important in dealing with any conflict.

Counselors often start with the premise that if there is difficulty between partners both are at fault. While each person has to deal seriously with this possibility, counselors and counselees need the ability to be able to deal with the possibility that both were *not* at fault. A husband we know wished to be reunited with his wife. He specifically took the blame for the break and asked his wife to disregard the pressure of the counselor to hold her accountable. This gave her the self-esteem and sense of fairness needed to forgive, which would have been more difficult if she had felt unfairly judged.

Most of us have at least one foot in childish reactions through much of our lives. We need to learn to let God love the little child within us. This child within needs to ask God to forgive its wrongdoing, and

Prosperity and Adversity

to ask for the ability to forgive others who have hurt it inadvertently or carelessly or selfishly. There is a story about an old man explaining love to a boy. "They (men) start at the wrong end of love. . . . Do you know how men should love? Love first a tree, a rock, a cloud."[4] In other words, people are the hardest to love. What the old man knew is a common discovery in marriage. We have boldly promised to love in prosperity and adversity and are woefully unprepared. This awareness can be discouraging. Here the slogan applies: "Be patient with me. God is not through with me yet."

If at any time we are satisfied with our marriage or with our children, we would have to be pompous fools not to think that luck and grace, rather than our own worth and efforts, were the causes. There is a real temptation for us to become smug when whatever plans we have work out. We all have the temptation to look down on those whose present plans seem to be failing. We have often in religious groups been in the presence of persons who could not understand that other people suffer much in their family life. Their own experience had been that hopes, dreams, and goals had been fulfilled. Indeed they attributed it to their religious behavior. They had trusted God and God had been faithful according to their "walk by sight" (2 Cor. 5:7). Logic would say that others who were stricken by adversity surely did not know their secret—the secret of their prosperity. We feel that although one would not seek adversity, one can seek the ability to learn from it. "May I be worthy of my trouble," someone has said. Even if we practice all of of the good habits and take a lifetime to learn them, it is God who gives the harvest.

DEALING WITH UNFULFILLED DREAMS

There is no promise that life will be stable and that idealistic pictures will be fulfilled. Yet we are disappointed when they are not. We do not expect our mates never to cause a ripple. Our children are certain to confound us—just as we did our parents. Childbirth is a passage that is cloaked with romanticism. The reality, if admitted, tells another story. It is a time of both physical and mental trauma. Each child produces a different environment in the home; each birth experience makes its own demands. Even if everything goes smoothly, it is still a trauma. Men as well as women need models to meet the challenge. For some, the two major adjustments of marriage and childbirth come close together. The new mother and father often feel like frightened children themselves. Coping with a new infant, though a healthy experience, is like coping with illness, for it debilitates the woman. Both parents need the love and support of family and the community. For some couples it may be the first real challenge to their relationship. Not every woman responds positively to motherhood. Not every father falls into the routine joyfully.

There is no way to know when we set out on the road of parenthood where it will end. Maturity in parents as well as their children comes at different stages in life. Also we may simply be better at some stages of parenting than at others. Most of us arrive safe and happy. Yet no one should fail to empathize with those who do not. We may be more fortunate than wise when children turn out well. Like the patriarch Abraham we are called to live out our lives in unknown territory.

Most of us think that if we have a "good Christian home," we will have good Christian children. So if we meet with adversity in the family we have a double pain—pain with our family and pain with our religion. We also have a double temptation—to deny the pain or to blame the partner.

When one partner takes the brunt of carrying the responsibility at a crisis time, that person may be in real danger of illness or even death. It is important for each person to take his or her share in working on the adversity and caring for the other. Both partners need to share the strains of the adversity and to monitor the other's health.

Next to a death in the family, careers have the largest effect upon marriages. Having a crisis or a disappointment in one's career is a great strain upon the marriage. Many men and women feel the sting of a disappointing career. If things do not work out, if jobs become uninspiring, or if a position with great promise fades into less than it seemed, creative energies are drained. Some form of disappointment comes into a wage earner's life, and the same can be true for volunteer work.

A way has to be found to regain enthusiasm and to create new energy. This getting back of lost energy may have to be intentional. Can we subject ourselves and our loved ones to our prolonged depression as we mope about how we have been treated? Maybe the dreams are outdated. Maybe our expectations have been unrealistic. More likely, circumstances which we had no way of predicting have come about.

Often a real assessment of our situation shows that if we have had one thing, having the other is unrealistic. Maybe the goal was not ours in the first place.

An exercise that may help you in this regard is to list your dreams. Mark them with an S for self, O for other, and C for culture, in order to tell where they came from. Then give them a positive or negative mark according to whether they have been helpful or unhelpful in your life. Is it time to quit evaluating yourself, your mate, or your child on the basis of attaining a dream which may not have been yours? Are you undervaluing them because of something our culture told you was of value?

INVESTMENT IN THE FUTURE

Our present way of living is an investment—for good or ill—in our future. We sow now in order to reap whenever there is the need to reap, even as we reap now whatever we have previously sown for this hour. The seeds of our aging, for example, are sown in young adulthood and through midlife. Healthy habits regarding eating and exercising tend to reap dividends in our later years. Healthy ways of coping with stress in our younger years are preventative of stress-related diseases in our later years. So also in regard to character habits. As we discipline ourselves to listen and to be sensitive to others in our young and middle years, this will carry over as we grow older. Unfortunately the same is true with unhealthy habits and self-centered attitudes.

By the same token practicing marriage *now* wherever you are in the life stage is a good investment for the future of your marriage—particularly for the possible hazards of prosperity and adversity. Keeping the communication channels between you and your spouse open *now* is the best assurance that they will be open at difficult times ahead. Practicing being supportive and sensitive in relating to your mate cannot begin too soon. Think of love as *loving:* building up the other; enjoying their presence and letting them know it; receiving, learning from the other, and expressing gratitude. This approach keeps the system open because it brings out the best in the partners. The first principle in conflict management is helping the other to feel good about himself or herself. It is a good principle for the prevention of conflict as well. People behave more lovingly and less defensively when they feel good about themselves than when they do not.

Two other principles of conflict management are pertinent to this practice of marriage also. First, strive for effective communication. This means listening to the other in order to know our mate, and sharing ourselves with the other that we may be known. Second, make a habit of honest and supportive ways of communicating. A good example of honest communication is marriage counselor Vera Mace, who, when she was asked whether she and her husband were ever angry with each other, replied, "Oh yes. But we have learned through the years how to deal with it. When I am angry with David, I say, 'David, I'm angry with you and I don't want to be. When can we talk about it?'"[5]

By repeatedly using this approach to anger in their marriage, the Maces were making a habit of good conflict management principles. Once this begins to happen they are more likely than not to follow this practice in moments of conflict or irritation. We are creatures of habit. Our freedom lies in *choosing* our habits.

If we are sensitive and loving in the little things we are likely also to be this way in the big things. Actually there are no little things to those who are experiencing them, although they may appear such to observers. They may even appear small in retrospect to those who were experiencing them. But at the time they were big. Since we are one flesh with our partner, what is big to one has to be big also to the other. *Wherever* a person is, *there* this person needs acceptance. In our petulant moments we may withhold this acceptance because our partner is not where we believe he or she should be. But since God does not do that with us, we can afford to come down from our pedestal of judgment and reach out to our partner where our partner is.

Once we do this we will begin to feel the other's pain. This is compassion—the most powerful healing influence in relationships. As Henri Nouwen says, "The beginning of healing is in our solidarity with the pain."[6] When you feel with your mate you will be inclined to be sensitive and supportive. So it is no surprise that compassion is one of the first of our positive capacities to dissipate when a marriage begins to sour. Hurt by the deterioration of the intimacy, we instead begin to feel only with ourselves.

While an inadequate financial base puts a great strain on a marriage and consistent money shortages create marital problems in and of themselves, the fact remains that it is those good gifts, like sensitivity and compassion, residing in our persons that make the difference between happiness and defeat in our relationships. And these cannot be procured by financial means. This is not to downplay the importance of those things that money can buy. Yet these cannot substitute for those reconciling qualities of the human spirit that are nurtured in a caring relationship—qualities that actually increase as they are exercised and experienced.

Both sensitivity and compassion are attributes of God's unconditional love that provides the security for the marital system. These are qualities of the spirit that are nurtured also by the nurturing community of the church, the extended family of the marriage. Here the love bond is focused in the reconciling power of the gospel. Built into the church fellowship is the compassion of the healing Christ.

Just the good conditioning of the body which comes from a healthy life style is no guarantee against illness and disease, so the good relational conditioning achieved through practicing marriage is no guarantee against marital crises. Both, however, are of help if such crises occur. Jack, for example, was in excellent physical condition, running fifty miles a week and swimming six. Yet in the prime of his life he suffered a heart attack. A stress-related job, a hereditary predisposition for the illness, and some fortuitous events all played their role. But what amazed the physician was Jack's rate of recovery. It was phenomenal. Here is where conditioning paid off.

In like manner, couples whose one-flesh relationship is in good condition are better able to deal with prosperity and adversity should these enter their lives. By keeping their channels of communication open through regular sharing and sensitive listening, they have developed their bond of friendship which provides the marital support for times of stress. With this heavy investment in their marriage, the partners are in a position to actualize the potential for growth that is inherent in the experience of adversity. Their relationship will continue to grow in and through the crises of their marital life.

As a couple, we needed the benefit of whatever we had done in practicing marriage for our difficult years. We both realize we could and should have done even more. We could have worked more directly on conflicts that were not pressing at the moment. Yet they were bound to become activated in full force during our adversity. We felt an incentive, then, to work through them because we knew we needed our relationship to see us through the difficult period. But we are grateful to God and to each other for the investment we *had* made. We now realize that practicing marriage needs to be its own incentive. Its purpose is sufficient in itself for the time and energy invested.

OUR MODEL NEXT DOOR

Early in our marriage we were very fortunate to have a neighboring couple who served as a good model for us. First of all, they were vitally interested in other people, their young neighbors included. Whereas they could have withdrawn socially into their own age group, they and their family became interested in the young couple next door. Observations of their frank, open relationship with each other have remained a vivid memory.

Van and Stan discussed each other with us on a positive realistic basis. In contrast to many marriages of that day, they were not manipulative or resigned to each other. In their conversations they communicated directly and clearly. Both of them could discuss matters thoroughly, giving their points of consideration without resorting to cute phrases or provocative language. Their anger was clear at times. It did not devastate either of them, nor did either shrug and give in. They did not speak in clichés or putdowns. If one mentioned a perceived failing of the other, he or she stated it without recriminations or bringing up the past. They both had the ability to be objective. Best of all they could do this in the presence of others.

One time, Lucy came to their porch and heard their raised voices. Van saw her. It was too late to leave. "Stanley, Lucy's here," she said. "I don't care if Lucy is here," Stanley shouted from within. "We're having an argument and we're going to finish. Come on in, Lucy!" They continued undisturbed, finally settling it to their satisfaction.

What would have embarrassed us even to speak about they could discuss. They illustrated, as well as we have ever seen, a closeness over the years.

After we had lived away from them many years we returned to be together with the family. Van had long been widowed. We asked Van how she could be in such radiant health, be working, and have such a positive outlook. She said simply, "Stanley was a good husband. He really cared for me." Their relationship was paying practical dividends even long after his death.

5
Cultivating Companionship

The marriage encounter movement uses the words "married singles" to describe persons who are married by law but not in life style. Either they are not ready for the kind of bonding that marriage requires or they are resisting it because they prefer a single life style.

DEMANDS OF MARRIAGE

There is no doubt that marriage makes demands on us. Bill can remember wailing loudly in the first few weeks of marriage, "I don't want to be a husband!" It was said and received in jest but looking back there was also a measure of truth to it. Life had become far more complicated with the new responsibility of sharing life totally with another.

When we marry we are no longer "our own." We belong instead to another whom we have to consider in making our plans and decisions. Ron found this a real problem in his marriage to Pat. He was used to doing things on his own since he left his parental home at age sixteen. For years he gave no account to anybody for his actions and he enjoyed the satisfaction of this kind of freedom. After going with Pat for only a few months, he was sure she was the one for him and was very effective in persuading Pat of the same.

Ron liked Pat as he liked the picture he had of marriage, picked up mostly from the media, and honestly believed he wanted to share life with her. But he did not realize what this meant. His own parents had only the minimal relationship needed to keep the family going. He had no models of what marriage required of him—such as informing Pat when he planned to return home, phoning her if his plans changed, or even consulting with her about his plans beforehand. When Pat complained, Ron agreed to be more accommodating but continued to keep her in the dark about his whereabouts. The issue finally became an emotional powder keg in their marriage. Fortunately they decided to seek counseling.

Sharing life with another may not come naturally. We have within us the desire to retain our independence. We do not like being obligated and resist belonging to another. Basically we are "loners." This is particularly true of the male in our culture. In this respect, we are following the American mystique of the independent frontier person—usually a man—who kept his thoughts and feelings to himself. Others could only guess what was going on behind the "poker face." The loner always remained in control of the situation. This model is more like the biblical character of John the Baptist than of Jesus. John was the loner prophet who lived a rugged and independent existence in the wilderness. Jesus lived with people in a closely knit community, and when feeling vulnerable, expressed his need for their support. Yet, even this comparison breaks down because John was willing to be eclipsed so that Jesus might be acclaimed.

In this loner mind-set people may like the idea of marriage better than the real thing, the romantic dimensions without the daily routines of life together, which can be quite unromantic at times. Our culture does not prepare us well for being married and we may resist it until the real thing begins to take hold.

Yet this real thing—belonging to another—is nothing new even for newlyweds. Our prior marriage to Christ contains the same kind of responsibility. This marriage can also meet resistance as we want instead to be obligated only to ourselves. In his response to this tendency, Saint Paul sets the record straight: "You are not your own, for you have been bought with a price" (1 Cor. 6:10).

In our egocentricity, however, we want to be our own—actually our own *god*. In the Garden of Eden story the serpent seduced the man and the woman from their commitment to the Creator by assuring them that, if they violated this commitment by eating of the fruit of the tree of the knowledge of good and evil, they would be as God. It was this desire—to be as God—that moved them to rebel. When they did rebel, they separated themselves not only from the Creator but also from each other. Each then wanted to be "their own." So when they had to face up to what they had done, each projected the blame: the man blamed the woman and the woman blamed the serpent (Genesis 3).

We recognize in this projection the familiar mentality that characterizes a culture of loners. This attitude—based primarily on being "one's own"—dissolves the bonds of community as each looks first to their own interests.

THE ILLUSION OF INDEPENDENCE

In spite of its frontier mystique, independence is an illusory symbol of freedom since it deprives us of the social satisfactions for which we were created. Independence *itself* is an illusion. What limited, fragile human being, who cannot be certain of being here tomorrow, can ever be independent? This is why the mystique requires its models to have superhuman controls. When personal resources give out or health deteriorates or our exercise of control no longer works, we realize all too painfully the illusion of self-sufficiency. Our resistance to facing our limits goes back again to the biblical story of the Fall. The attraction to being one's own god is based on the resistance to accepting human limitations. Through Christ, the Creator has brought us back to our origin. The price of that redemption—the cross—means we are no longer our own. Belonging to another is native to our identity as humans. Our freedom lies in being who we are—limited and vulnerable and dependent on God. As the old hymn puts it, "Make me a captive, Lord, and then I shall be free." The paradox of these words parallels Jesus' saying that we find ourselves only by losing ourselves in service to God—and that if we seek only to save or protect ourselves, we shall lose even what we have (Luke 17:33).

The demands of being married complicate things for us so that we can feel overwhelmed and trapped by them. Within this perspective the bond of belonging to another becomes a chain. There is another perspective, however, in which belonging to another is the way to fulfillment, the way by which human freedom is realized.

THE MODEL OF INTERDEPENDENCE

The mutuality of belonging that characterizes being married is based on the biblical model of interdependence. The marital relationship structured on this interdependence model is a paradigm of community.

This mutuality of belonging provides endurance to the relationship. It is the real thing in being married, which also gives real freedom. The mutuality of giving and receiving promotes the stimulus for both the marriage relationship and the marital partners to grow. On the other hand, where one partner is the giving one and the other the receiving one, the relationship is stymied along with the partners.

The marriage of Beverly and Dan is an example of such imbalance. Dan is the problem—he knows it and so does everybody who knows him. Beverly is a fixer, a problem solver. Perhaps it was these contrasting qualities that drew them together. But it was not good bonding because each became locked into their positions. After awhile Dan tired of being the problem. "It's hard being married to someone who has it all together," he said. It *is* hard—on one's self-esteem! The caregiver has the status, not the care receiver.

The interdependence needed for a healthy one-flesh relationship is related by Saint Paul to the sexual dimension of marriage. "The husband," he said, "should give to his wife her conjugal rights and likewise the wife to her husband. For the wife does not rule over her own body, the husband does, likewise the husband does not rule over his own body, but his wife does" (1 Cor. 7:4). Note the mutuality of the woman in marital intimacy even in an age of male domination, specifically in matters of sex. This domination is still with us. In contrast, Saint Paul's description is a remarkable affirmation of the mutuality and interdependence of husbands and wives, and also of their equality in the intimacy of their relationship.

COMPANIONSHIP IN MIDLIFE

"Midlife" is a term used with considerable flexibility. Let us assume for our purposes that midlife still comes at age forty to forty-five. We are speaking of the time when careers and children are settled issues and there is less mystery about the future. Adjustment to parenthood and the realities of multiple responsibilities has taken place. It is now time to prepare for the years ahead as seriously as one prepared for marriage, career, and parenthood. This stage, however, though no less crucial, gets little attention.

Well-adjusted middle-aged couples seldom see themselves for what they are—mentors for young couples. Young couples can look about them and see which couples have become what they would like to be.

Cultivating Companionship

The parents of one of our friends were people who enjoyed life in an era when jokes and comic strips often portrayed marriage as a trap. They were thrilled to go out together, pleased that they were creating a home together. Once when we were going to lunch with them and they were holding hands, the woman turned to us and said, "Daddy and I still date." It was obvious then and still is, now that they are in their eighties, that these people valued their marriage.

Middle age is a good stage for looking forward to later years. What can we do to assure a happy and healthy future, now expanded by our new longevity? Church leaders who design programs for members' needs should keep in mind the need for future planning at midlife.

Middle age is analogous to the adolescent stage in many ways. The adolescent is defining himself or herself in order to enter the adult stage. Parents can be aware of this natural progress and furnish the adolescent feedback so that entering the adult world is not such a shock. If the adolescent is surly in actions, he or she can begin to see and be responsible for the results of this personality choice. In contrast, in middle age it is our own observations instead of a parent's, which provide feedback with both amusement and pity.

New questions can be raised. "Is it so important to make it?" "Are my reactions defensive?" "Do I really want to spend the rest of my life in the manner which may not ensure my future happiness and growth?" Insecurity may make us unduly worried about arriving at our goals on time. As a child, Lucy remembers always being in a hurry. When she would turn a test in, her teachers frequently asked, "Did you look on the back of the page?" In her haste to get through she rushed past the latter questions. In middle age, we are, in effect, looking on the back of the page. Instead of brushing these questions aside, they can now be viewed with excitement. In midlife we tend to evaluate ourselves with the labels of success and failure. Yet we really may not know what *is* success and failure. What we do know is that unproductive personality traits need to be challenged. Rather than feeling out of control in midlife, for some this time is the best opportunity they have to achieve a new power of choice. It may take some time for *both* of the partners to work through this challenge.

To meet these challenges, it is important to become more in tune with our "adult" person. Our new relationships may include our children's mates and even their parents. Our relationship with our own parents may "turn over" during this time, and we may need to take care of *them*. Our career development may also include more responsibility. Lucy, for example, had to learn to be more assertive in social interchange for her own satisfaction. Any such added responsibility makes it necessary to be clear with mate, family, friends, and colleagues about one's own needs.

During middle age the partners need to work together in the changes before them. Youth is traditionally a time to try our wings. Although we may always be trying our wings, by midlife some of these ventures are ready to be set aside so that we can concentrate on whatever is most realistic for our own situation. Marriage has its specific realisms in midlife. For example, shared parenting may not have been a mutually happy experience. The partners may not have been well matched in their attitudes and interests as parents.

In midlife when intensive parenting usually ends, couples need to come to peace with whatever differences they have had in their parenting roles lest these negatively color future relationships. Recently when a couple visited to meet our new grandchild, the man voiced a bitter regret that they had only one child. "How I would love to have a son!" he said. It was cruel in the fact that the wife is beyond childbearing. From the conversation I was sure the regret was new and unexpected. These people will not be thrown off balance by this, however. The wife said quietly, "It is too late for that," and went on with the visit.

Men and women who in the past had to choose between career and parenting may now feel bitterness. In midlife the bitterness which one partner can heap upon the other needs to be seen in light of past hurts. What is needed now is forgiveness and healing. Both can help each other to find satisfaction in the later stages of parenting, which may be as important and creative as earlier stages. Nor is it too late to pursue challenges outside the home.

If people are serious about finding satisfaction in middle age they know that they have to grow. For example, if a man desires his wife at this time to look her best he should not saddle her with all of the responsibility of the home to the extent that she feels like a drudge. If a woman wants a decisive husband but consistently finishes his sentences and makes unilateral decisions, she may not have such a husband at midlife.

There is recognized charm in the stage of adolescence. Parents may often wonder what kind of adults will develop from these adolescents.

One could have the same question about middle age. Even so, a married person who attempts to make changes in himself or herself can expect to make waves in the marital relationship. In the one-flesh relationship, changes in one partner necessitate changes in the other. Open discussion of one's wishes and dreams may not draw an overjoyed response. But it can lead to new shared activities when a commitment is made to take a small step in the direction of satisfaction. For example, having both partners join a self-exploratory group can be truly rewarding. It was our privilege a decade ago to explore the human potential movement together. We treasure those times. Church groups often offer opportunities for spiritual and personal exploration.

CARING FOR OLDER PARENTS

This is a time for mates to be close. More middle-aged couples today have parents who are still living because of increased longevity. Seventy-year-old children with parents in their nineties are becoming more common. Sometimes a marriage that functioned well most of the time founders on the issue of care for elderly parents. One person trying to make all of the decisions will not lead to marital satisfaction. Each individual needs to work out an acceptance of the situation.

The relationship to one's parents may need practical reassessment. Nowhere is there more unfinished business; nowhere is objectivity more illusive. While we are not responsible for our parents' behavior, we are responsible if we are introducing negative stimuli into the relationship. Relationships with siblings are also crucial as the time when aging parents will need help draws near. The family needs to be in accord with any decisions regarding the parents to avoid trouble. As they do this they are providing a good model for their children to follow in the future. Then the future, no matter what care is needed, is approached in a helpful way.

If parents over the years have undercut a daughter-in-law or son-in-law or even a son or daughter, they cannot be surprised when that person is not enthused about helping to plan for their care. Middle age is the time to become fair about what you can do for others and also fair to yourself. A man who always accepts the "John doesn't mind doing it" role may find that he wants to redefine his position. "I like to help, but when it is not my turn and I have a conflict, I say so."

It would be easy if all responsibility for parents were removed but it is not possible even in our day; every generation has had to accept its responsibilities in varying degrees. There are persons who cannot fit into our conventional care for the elderly.

Neighbors of ours showed wisdom when they were looking for a larger home for their growing boys. They sought property and found it within a comfortable radius of their aging parents' home. The children now do the chores of mowing and shoveling which the grandparents cannot do. Their children will learn that caring for parents is expected and dignifying.

Other acquaintances of ours who had no children enriched the lives of their nieces and nephews, providing trips, handmade clothing, and encouragement. Their beautiful fiftieth wedding party was a loving gift of these nieces and nephews. These nieces and nephews have been providing much support to this couple during their recent years of illness. By resisting negative feelings and caustic comments and by building up others with encouraging support instead, we may reap a pleasant harvest of love and care in our own later years. There are no guarantees of such an outcome, but we will at least not have blocked the impulse for caring for others.

People in midlife often desire a time of peace and quiet to enjoy the benefits of their labor. We were surprised at midlife to find that parenting remains a large part of our lives and always will. Only the emphasis changes. As we progress beyond midlife to face more challenges, we are grateful for all the opportunities for growth available today that our parents' generation did not have. The question "What do I know that I resist knowing?" is often answered—to our benefit.

SEXUAL COMPANIONSHIP

The joy of a maturing marriage draws the partners to each other in love and affection. The sexual communion of marriage is essentially a celebration of the relationship. Companionship is a stimulus to sexual desire. This is particularly true when this companionship includes the sharing of what is going on within one's mind and heart. As we reveal ourselves to the other we feel close, intimate with the other. The sharing has *joined* us.

In a study conducted among male clergy and their spouses, the sexual desire of the wives tended to be less than that of their husbands, which was a concern for both. From other sections of the study it was

Cultivating Companionship

evident that this contrast was not due to any physiological differences. In the responses, it was clear that these same wives felt that their husbands could be more helpful in the tasks of managing home and family. They were also more aware than their husbands of problems in the family or in the marriage. The men, on the other hand, were more involved in their work than with their families, and had less time for marital companionship than the wives desired.[1]

It is doubtful that these marriages of clergy are much different from marriages of laypeople. Women tend to be more sensitive to the need for a total relationship than are men, while men are more likely to put most of their time and energy into their work. The result is that each may approach the sexual relationship in their marriage from differing perspectives. When the hand that reaches out for sexual intimacy is also the hand that has been supportive and caring throughout the relationship, it is likely to meet with a response in kind; how different is the response where there has been a failure to provide this support and caring. Intercourse that is solely or even primarily sexual ceases to be an intercourse between persons.

This personal understanding of intercourse is shown in the biblical verb for sexual intimacy, "to know." This word in its biblical context means to know a person rather than a fact. Joseph, for example, "knew her [Mary] not until she had borne a son [Jesus]" (Matt. 1:25). When it is understood in this context, sexual intercourse is actually a celebration of personal intercourse. So if there is to be a genuine celebration there needs to be something to celebrate. When the personal intercourse is lacking, women in particular may not find sexual intercourse that desirable.

One of the advantages of the maturing process is that we become increasingly liberated from cultural pressures to prove ourselves in what we do—specifically in sex. Are we good in bed? Good at satisfying the other? Are we sexually potent? Sexually liberated? Sexually passionate? Genuine liberation would include being liberated from these "standards" of qualification so that we can grow in our acceptance of the pleasures of sex for their own sake as a gift of God.

Sexual intercourse in marriage is a reflection of the Eucharist in our prior marriage with Christ. Eucharist means thanksgiving. The sacrament of the Eucharist (Communion), therefore, is a celebration of the gifts we have received in the great adventure of being married to

Christ. Even as we do not focus on our "performance" in the Eucharist, but rather on the reassurance of love and acceptance that is being dramatized and tangibly expressed in the sacrament, so "performance consciousness" in sexual intimacy blocks our participation in the drama of lovemaking.

Sexual desire is by its very nature subject to fluctuation. Life itself is a fluctuation, an ebb and flow, that is at times understood and at times not. Changes are constantly taking place—in body chemistry, in personal experiences, in day-by-day living—and these changes affect sexual desire in different ways for different people. Those entering into marriage may not be prepared for these fluctuations. Instead they may have visions of marriage as a sexual panacea. This image is encouraged by the media displays of sexual intimacies: pictures and descriptions of beautiful bodies naked together in warm comfortable surroundings, rollicking in bed in total ecstasy. It is an image that does not correspond to the realities of day-by-day living together—of fluctuating moods, tired bodies, and anxious minds. If we can learn in the early years of marriage to temper this image with reality, we will make the best of both our romantic aspirations and the fluctuations that seem to frustrate them.

By midlife, however, we might again be grasping at romantic images as a way of resisting the realities of aging. As a symbol of life, sexuality with all of its energies may again become a way of measuring up. Only now the question is "Do I still have it—virility, sex appeal?" The media model becomes the judge of one's performance. "How was it?" means "How did I do?" "How often?" means "How often are we really living?" "Do I qualify as a real man—woman?" "Am I sexy—a skillful lover?"

All of these questions indicate the basic anxiety behind them. Sex is judging us, instead of our enjoying sex. When we can temper the media image with the realities of a fluctuating existence, we can focus our attention where it belongs—on the relationship. "How is our sex life?" is a healthy question only when it is accompanied by the more basic question, "How is our relationship?" Instead of focusing on how we are celebrating, we can focus instead on what we are celebrating.

It is customary to stress the role of the "child" in us with reference to sex. Since children can abandon themselves to pleasure without having to use it for ulterior purposes, the "child" obviously needs to

Cultivating Companionship

dominate in sex. But the "parent" within us is needed also to provide the blessing of authority on the experience. Also the "adult" within us is needed in order to provide objectivity to the experience. The pleasure is physical but also spiritual; it is knowing another within the bond of a covenant.

Wanting sex and wanting the partner may be two different things. We are recognizing now that some people are addicted to sex. Sex is a symbol of the interdependence of the one-flesh relationship. For the addict, however, the symbol becomes separated from the relationship and no longer communicates that which it symbolizes. The person with whom one has sex is less important than what the sexual sensations have come to represent. Having sex becomes an antidote to loneliness, an assurance of love. But it is a false antidote because it bypasses the personal. The other is used, rather than related to. Sex as an addiction is like getting a "fix"—it temporarily stills the anxiety and dulls the pain of rejection.

Marital partners need to cultivate the sexual stimulation of the whole person. In Paul Tournier's terms, they need to relate to the "person" behind the "personage."[2] The personage is what we perceive of the other through our senses, including the other's sexual manifestations. The personage, however, may or may not reveal the person. Too often we try to hide our person behind false impressions. But in the intimacy of marital companionship the person is revealed—here and there, now and then—and when this happens our appreciation, acceptance, and love for the person comes forth in sexual desire. Where the personage in its falsification can ultimately turn the other off, the person by stimulating in the other compassion and care, turns him or her on. Being married is then understood experientially.

Because of the orientation of our sexual nature to our total person, dialogue is of utmost importance to the marital relationship. It is through dialogue that companionship flourishes, and the way is cleared for celebrating this dialogue sexually.

In our busy schedules we may need to schedule time just for each other, time for no other purpose than sharing where we are and how we feel in the relationship. Fifteen minutes for sharing may be all we can manage on some days but it will prove more qualitatively valuable than its limited time would indicate. Mutuality in sharing is reinforced if the partners take turns initiating the dialogue. Suggestions for conversation can be prepared for the next time. Marriage Encounter encourages couples to practice this kind of daily dialogue through letters. For ourselves, a less fixed structure for dialoguing is desirable. Couples will need to find their own form of expression. Regular dialogue helps each partner to grow in appreciation of the relationship, which in turn provides more reason for celebrating.

In its holistic understanding, sexual intercourse is a nutrient uniquely designed for the marital relationship. Again it was Saint Paul who understood this. Marital partners, he advised, should not refuse one another in marital intimacy. An exception would be for them to devote themselves to prayer. But even this exception should be by mutual consent and of short duration. But then, he adds, "come together again lest Satan tempt you through lack of self-control" (1 Cor. 7:5-6). While the apostle may be thinking largely of the problems caused by sexual frustration, his insights on marriage go beyond that. He sees the stabilizing influence of sexual intimacy for marriage. He also sees the mutuality or equality of men and women in the decisions regarding this intimacy. These are rather amazing insights on the part of one who has been accused of being locked into patriarchal views of marriage.

SENSITIVITY IN SEX

Sexual communication remains an important part of life well past midlife. One can tell by conversations with middle-aged people how it is with them. There may be an awkward, oblique reference to lack of satisfaction, a wife's or husband's lack of respect for the other, or curiosity about another's sex life, which gives away the pain.

The middle-aged or older woman needs the affirmation of sexual love. Among the attitudes which prevent good sexual communication is lack of forgiveness. Neither husband nor wife can afford to let old slights, past hurts, and past mistakes go unforgiven. As husbands and wives see each other as interesting, vulnerable, and fresh, they enter into a continually new sexual relationship. Just as you cannot step into the same river, so you cannot have the same sexual experience. The message from each intercourse should be one of hope for the future and pleasure for the present. Intercourse gives the message that two people are able to satisfy and affirm each other.

After menopause a woman needs to have sexual intercourse to be able to continue doing so into old age. The man can help in this regard

Cultivating Companionship

by his spiritual and mature attitude toward her, and by maintaining a cheerful and positive approach toward sexuality by being attentive, expressing gratitude, and giving tokens of caring. Such tokens, when they are selected according to the man's knowing of his spouse and her tastes, are highly prized. Attractiveness now is in the spirit as well as in the body. Yet, a happy remark that expresses attraction, one that brightens one's day, is worth more than a large gift. No woman asks for such reinforcements but she misses them if she does not get them and envies the woman who does. To make a time and a place for sexual communication to happen is more important in midlife than before. The sexual relationship will last when it is valued.

When we do workshops for couples, we ask them to divide into separate groups and to brainstorm ways to keep "lover-ness" in marriage. By "lover-ness" we mean the quality in a marriage that keeps the man and woman as lovers. The couples can be as silly as they desire and think both big and small. It is interesting that their lists never contain more than a few items that require money. The few exotic things that are sprinkled in indicate that these couples appreciate the sensual side of marriage. Young couples hear how the older couples keep lover-ness going in their marriage and older ones learn new ways to please their spouse.

Nothing can become more stale than one person always waiting for the other to act. Negative feelings get generated before anything can begin. In lovemaking it is especially so. Acting on one's feelings, not waiting for the other to do so, adds a new stimulus to sexual intimacy. Acceptance and entering in are appreciated by the initiator. Most of us go through times in our lives when it is hard to demonstrate affection: times when jobs require excessive attention, times of illness, and other major life disruptions.

While one must live within the rhythm of such disruptions, we need to return to the rhythm of marital affection as the norm of practicing marriage. Ours alone is the story of our life, no matter how much we learn from others' experiences or relate to the similar experiences of others. The unique nature of the one-flesh companionship makes the story of each marriage an epic adventure!

6
Growing Older Together

Growing older *together* is a potentially positive adventure because *growing older* is a potentially positive adventure. This is not what we usually hear or expect to hear. Ours is an anti-aging culture and the prospects for the aging process are considered downhill all the way. In fact, we program ourselves this way. We expect to become physically decrepit and shoved to the side as older persons. Unfortunately this very expectation can influence what actually happens. Then we may "discover" that what we had anticipated is so. Self-fulfilling prophecies occur in our aging as well as other aspects in our life.

COPING WITH AGEISM

Literary critic Malcolm Cowley, in his eighties, says that "we start by growing old in other peoples' eyes and then slowly we come to share their judgment."[1] The word "old" has a stigma connected with it in our culture. Being old means being out of it so far as where the action is. The word "old" thus actually expresses an *attitude* toward aging. For this reason we prefer to use the words "growing *older* together." Growing older is a process we all participate in all the time. It takes away the judgment associated with a particular time of life.

The attitude toward aging is different in other cultures, particularly Third World cultures. At advanced age these people come into their prime. They acquire status and influence as older persons. This shows that it is not aging as such that is negative. Rather, a prejudice known as *ageism* rejects aging and all that goes with it in favor of youth and young adulthood.

Though it is difficult to do in our culture, you *can* program yourself and your marriage positively as you envision the senior years. Those who refuse to buy into this negative perspective are the healthier among us. As one senior put it, "I've been too involved with the things I'm doing to realize that I am aging." You and your spouse can say with the poet Browning, "Grow old with me, the best is yet to be." And it could well be! You can continue to grow as persons as long as you live. You can also watch and guide your spouse into paths of growth so that you grow *together*. As in that verse, growing older, besides being a positive adventure, is an experience to share with another. Our growth needs to take place within our marriage rather than apart from it.

Soren Kierkegaard warned that one can grow away from something as well as toward something as one grows older.[2] Our culture seems to say the same thing. Older years mark our displacement from the mainstream of societal living to the periphery. We are changed from people with a present and future into people with a past. But Kierkegaard meant something far different from this. He meant that we could lose the vision, the idealism, the integrity often characteristic of young people. He had seen too many people stifle their individuality and their convictions in order to adjust to the cultural mores. They become "ciphers in the crowd" ground "smooth as pebbles" by the need to conform and to fit.

Perhaps you also have seen this happen to people. We have seen it happen to marriages. We have on occasion renewed old acquaintances after many years with couples whom we remembered as young marrieds, obviously in love and eager for living. Now, however, they seem to have lost their spark and are preoccupied with self-centered concerns, obsessed with their need for security. The pains and disappointments they have obviously experienced over the years, rather than being stimuli for marital and personal growth, have evidently instead been stimuli for cynicism and bitterness. It is sad—when we realize what might have been!

But neither our culture's perception of aging nor Kierkegaard's perception of the loss of youthful idealism needs to take place. Instead we can grow *toward* something as we age. Neither of the above grim realities is the way that God designed the aging or maturing process according to the Scriptures. In contrast, the older years are to be respected. "You shall rise up before the hoary head and honor the face of an old man" (Lev. 19:32).

Our bodies slow down as do our minds as we go through the senior years, but not to the extent that people in our culture anticipate. Older people take more time than younger people to return to normal after exercising, for example. In this as in other differences, however, some eighty-year-olds show no more decline than the average fifty-year-old. Many of us think of the elderly as residents of nursing homes. Yet only 5 percent of the elderly are in these homes. Most of the elderly are leading active and interdependent lives.

Even though there is a slowing down in our natural abilities in our later years, the capacity of our spirit actually expands. As Saint Paul describes this paradox, "Though our outer nature is wasting away, our inner nature is being renewed every day" (2 Cor. 4:16). So far as Paul is concerned this is more than enough compensation. Psychiatrist Fritz Kunkel sees it similarly: "Every loss in the realm of the natural life could and should be an adequate gain in the realm of the spirit."[3]

The older years are times of increasing limits. Yet this is really nothing new; accepting limits goes with being human. We may experience more limits as we age. The biggest gain from these losses, however, would be an increasing ability to accept ourselves as we are. If this should happen we can become more free from the cultural demands on us to prove something—our worth, our manhood, our womanhood, our competence, our success, our popularity, or whatever. By the later years the "score" is more likely to be in. Then with fewer images to live up to, we are freer to choose our own identity as persons and as a married couple, and to enjoy today with each other.

Though our productivity, culturally speaking, may be curtailed in later years, largely through arbitrary retirements, we can continue to grow in spirit—as persons, as a relationship—as the years add their accumulation of learning. This learning includes learning to know and appreciate our spouse in ways not possible before. We grow in our sensitivity to the other and our empathy enables us to relate more intimately. Knowing, appreciating, and relating to each other are neverending challenges. Practicing marriage produces personal qualities that probably await this stage in living for their development.

Except for times when we shut each other out during a conflict, we have always believed that we had a "good marriage." As we look back we still concur with that judgment. Yet in doing an exercise at a marital enrichment seminar in which we were asked to mention something distinctive about our marriage, we became aware, almost as a surprise, that our present distinction is that we are getting along better than at any time previously. After forty years of marriage! The later stages of life have a lot to offer.

There is a wisdom that comes only from living—a learning that comes only from experience. As someone has said, "Youth is a gift of nature. Aging is a work of art." The key to learning from experience is our openness to forgive and be forgiven. If we can face up to our mistakes, our wrong decisions, and our sins, we are less likely to repeat them.

The religious word for this facing up to our faults is "repentance." It means literally to change our minds. Knowing that we are forgiven because God has assured us of this in our covenant of baptism, we can come to terms with our defensiveness. What is there to defend when we are forgiven? So we learn through much pain and joy to drop our defenses and own up to who we are. We can see in this potential the pivotal role of the gospel in effecting change in our persons and in our marriage. We learn from our experiences only after we come to peace with them. It is then that they become a source of wisdom.

The alternative is obstructive defensiveness and subsequent repression of the learning potential. This is what Kierkegaard saw could happen to people as they grew older. They become defensive because of the pain of facing reality—the threat to their self-image if they are revealed to be something less than perfect—the bad taste of guilt over their behavior. When they deny actions or defend them, they obviously have less conscious pain, but they become also less of a person, which ultimately leads to *more* pain.

God's reconciling overtures through Christ make it possible for us to learn from our day-to-day living, since we are relieved from having to defend ourselves against the judgments that this living entails. As those who are reconciled with themselves because they are reconciled to God, we can reflect on these day-by-day experiences with our marriage and allow them to enhance our knowledge of life—which includes knowledge and appreciation of our mate.

CONTINUING TO LEARN, GIVE, GROW

God's covenant of forgiveness makes the difference between learning from experience and replaying our old tapes. These tapes contain our patterns for meeting life's experiences. When they are unsatisfactory and need to be replaced, forgiveness allows us to do it; we have a method by which the old tapes can be replaced by a new set which produces positive results. Forgiveness allows us to stop unproductive actions to which guilt and fear have made us prone. We learn to mend our ways because we acknowledge that we are on the wrong track.

If we are sincere about looking at life as a journey to understand ourselves and others, we can change. The purpose of Luther's words, "sin bravely," is to lead us toward improved actions and away from arrogant attitudes about our actions; "that's the way I am, I can't really do differently, nor do I wish to." A family often accepts this kind of power play, since those involved go through this routine unconsciously. A marriage with such insensitivity present, and without any acknowledgment of wrongdoing, becomes intolerable.

When retirement and close association brings the couple more time together than has ever been possible, certain behaviors become very irritating. Previously these irritations may have been tolerated, but now the behavior needs to change. A man or woman used to treating others as inferior may have a rude awakening when he or she discovers that this manner must be changed. We have talked to several retired elementary-school teachers whose husbands have made humorous statements about being treated as school kids. Similarly, the wife of a man in charge of a few employees whom he was used to bullying stated that she could not endure his kind of abuse and putdown all day long.

As was pointed out before, retirement at sixty or seventy has a new meaning when it may last for more than twenty years. Retirement should be more a period for growth than a prolonged rest stop. We will need to find ways to keep relationships growing and satisfactory. This will involve us in confrontation, change, and forgiveness. Persons who have gone through this progression to more satisfying relationships than they have had before, have an experience of marital refreshment equal to none! Even physical health and sexual health are regenerated.

Some churches and communities are taking the lead by having seminars and workshops that address the problems of retirees. Learning to relate to each other within the marriage is of course the best way to ensure that retirement years do not become a tangled web of confusing situations. Getting together with other couples to share insights is a very broadening experience. In like manner we receive enlightenment in our faith as we meet together to worship and to participate in other activities of the church. We are fortunate that such good opportunities are available.

In the retirement years a parent may become the victim of his or her own strong-minded child. If, however, that parent has had the opportunity to grow during his or her retirement years, the strong-minded child is handled more effectively. In fact, the parent may even help this adult child to overcome an irritating habit of bossiness. Resistance to any manipulation by children who may have returned home or with whom one must live is healthy. The goal is to be congruent *ourselves*—to accept ourselves and to act in a manner which expresses our real selves. This involves using energy to find one's own center so that one can give direct messages, thus saving the energy usually spent in defensiveness. There is less possibility then of being harmful to others. This also means being more accepting and less judging of others.

Older people have more data and experience to work with, but using these resources wisely depends upon the motive and the will to grow. The person who does not continue to grow becomes tiresome in his or her conversation, "unattuned" to the present, and therefore unhelpful to others. One needs to see each situation as fresh and new so that one's contribution to society, no matter how small, comes from responsible thinking as long as one lives.

When we learn from our mistakes and act upon our insights, others are less likely to take us for granted. Relationships will remain fresh and not predictable. While there is "nothing new under the sun," there is also no limit to the varieties of our experiences. Because of the very extent of our experiences we may tend to compare new situations to the past and therefore miss the freshness in them. Older people need to guard against minimizing the importance of any present opportunity. They will then not become bored with life's apparent repetitions and in turn will not bore others. As we grow older together in this kind of adventuresome spirit, we can remain exhilarated in our anticipations. Something *is* going to happen if we have not already written it off. Older couples who meet life in this spirit enrich society by serving as good models.

Indeed people who have learned the secret of being "alive and aware" cannot find satisfaction in relationships that do not proceed in a dynamic way. Hearing mature people discuss their vulnerability openly, admitting to faults and disappointing outcomes, is much better than the alternative of repeating words and actions that are obviously destructive to our relationships. As we grow older we need others' feedback to our behavior even more than before because we are more inclined to defend ourselves and our past—perhaps since there is more to defend. At the same time, as older persons we could be more capable of reasoned actions because of this larger backlog of experience.

Culturally we have only recently made structural, institutional adjustments to the fact of aging. People have always sought support from informal groups such as church groups, however. The need for financial planning was probably the impetus for current seminars on aging. We have always been aware of the need for preparing for the time when we can no longer earn our necessities by working. Advances in medical knowledge together with the specialized study of gerontology have brought us more complete information about the needs of older people. We now know there is a connection between our physical well-being and our emotional and spiritual growth.

Hopefully this improved knowledge of the needs of older people can lead both older parents and their adult children to more open and tolerant actions toward each other. It was said of the eighty-plus mother of one of our friends, "She says what she thinks when she thinks it." There were times when her frank comments had hurt others, but the over-all effect was positive. Her children do not know what she is likely to say, nor can they take her for granted. She does not ask them to make sacrifices that would be harmful to them, nor does she spare them her evaluations and suggestions. In turn, her children do not keep things from her and speak freely to her as they would with their own peers. She is involved in any mutual decisions and can be counted on for a congruent answer without any hint of manipulation. Those who know her love her.

In our observations, one of the limiting factors in living arrangements for older people is the lack of acceptance of relying upon outside help. We have had this situation with both Bill's father and Lucy's mother. Both of them could have stayed in their own homes longer if they had been comfortable with a nonfamily member coming in. Some social agencies are trying to match older people who need some service with students and other adults who would like a free room or lower rent. Older people who have developed their interrelational skills can best accept this arrangement. This not only applies to older persons who are living alone but applies equally to older couples who wish to remain in their home. If they are able to express satisfaction and to confront unsatisfactory conditions without undue stress, they can accept these arrangements that enable them to stay in their home longer.

The situation today of career women who are marrying later is similar to the situation into which we were born. Both of us were born when our parents were past thirty. When we were in our years of heaviest parental responsibility, our own parents retired. When they needed care, we still had children in the home. Unlike those who were feeling the squeeze of both parents and grandchildren, we were involved with parenting our own children in a crucial way. One advantage of this was that we were not reminded as much of our own coming infirmity. Our friends who are in their sixties and caring for parents who are in their eighties and nineties, express intensified feelings of depression over aging. Their energy is also often limited so that they must find outside help to cope with the conditions of their own and their parents' infirmity. The joy of seeing several generations together can evaporate if the couple in their sixties feels overburdened with too much family responsibility. It is important for couples caught in this dilemma to continue practicing marriage lest their own relationship be squeezed dry.

A person such as Maggie Kuhn has modeled the kind of responsibility that older people are uniquely capable of assuming. In founding the Gray Panthers she has taken up advocacy for the elderly and for world peace. We parents are concerned about our children's future. Having nuclear weapons in place and the fear of accidents from them, not to mention the threat of nuclear war itself, has made activists out of many older people. They realize they can do something for their children's and grandchildren's future.

Betty Bumpers, wife of Senator Dale Bumpers of Arkansas, at sixty-one is very active in the organization which she started in 1982, Peace Links. She realized that her daughter's and grandchild's future could be endangered. More than one hundred bipartisan congressional wives have helped Mrs. Bumpers to involve women on peace issues. This time they are working "not for their husbands, but for their children." Most of these women have no history of political activism. Mrs. Bumper's organization serves the valuable function of giving information from peace groups to anyone who wants it. As she says, "Mutually assured destruction is not good enough for me."[4] Dr. Benjamin Spock is another who is using his mature years for peace advocacy.

As we have a larger capacity for understanding due to our years of experience, we who are older can make the effort to become well informed, and thus earn the right as well as the duty to speak out. There are many opportunities today for older people to continue their education through universities (reduced tuition) and other community education programs through which they can also increase their effectiveness in speaking and writing. This is a great couple adventure!

BACK TO WHERE WE STARTED

Once when a chairwoman was encouraging us volunteers to tackle a hard job she said, "The reward for doing a job well is the ability to do a harder one." When we challenge ourselves we will learn to do more; when we do not challenge ourselves our abilities will not increase. The choice is ours.

A former junior high school in our neighborhood has become a center for adult education. Adults of any age may earn a G.E.D. There are also classes for seniors in square dancing, for learning crafts, and even the arrangement for selling these crafts at a boutique. In its swimming pool I have met people who have learned to swim after retirement. One of them said, "I am tired of paying medical bills for those who do not take care of themselves." While one cannot on a one-to-one basis equate illness with lack of exercise or poor diets, or accidents with careless driving (there are classes for seniors to brush up on driving skills), these poor habits do have some relationship to these afflictions. The benefit of working to remain healthy and to avoid accidents is the feeling of being in control—and in the case of marriage, the feeling of doing it also for the other. *We* both appreciate each other's efforts in this direction.

Some of our dearest dreams and wishes may not come true. We may suffer from our own mistakes and not all of them can be turned into positive effects. We are probably like many of you who are reading this. We and many of our couple friends have suffered heavy losses. Even if we practice all of the good habits and take a lifetime to learn them, it is God who gives the harvest. We cannot reduce our world completely to the predictability of cause and effect. Unreal expectations and regrets will only impede our ability to cope realistically with life. The present will give us opportunities, and we will be happier if we take them. We can still help our mate to feel alive by voicing our appreciation for his or her presence.

T. S. Eliot said,

> We shall not cease
> From exploration.
> The end of all our exploring
> Will be to arrive where we started
> And know the place
> For the first time.[5]

In the later stages of marriage we are back to where we started. Love and commitment rather than children or other pursuits are again the glue of the marriage. The challenge of developing careers and the rearing of children are for all practical purposes finished chapters, but the sustaining motif of the marriage is the same love and commitment with which we began. "The more things change, the more they remain the same." The vows are not changed as we age. They speak of practicing affection and concentrating on each other's growth for as long as we live. The past instructs us and we take what joy we can from it, appreciating our memories.

Humor is a wonderful quality to find in the later years, since humor makes contemporaries of everyone. Laughter brings a feeling of warmth and identification. Some years ago we called upon a friend's parents while on sabbatical leave. We expected to make just a short perfunctory call but we received a great blessing. First, the husband showed us his yard. We are gardeners, so we could appreciate his skill and expertise. Espaliered fruit trees, pruned berry bushes, sculptured hedges were all tastefully placed on a small city lot. Inside, the hostess brought out a clipping file, and selected some to read. Soon we were wiping our eyes helplessly. She had collected humorous events from the paper for many years. They were new to us and she had been blessed with a wonderful sense of the ridiculous. These people became treasures to us for several years. Later, they gracefully moved across the country to be with their own son and daughter-in-law, where they quickly made new friends. They were spiritually and physically present to themselves and others. You could not meet them without enjoying them. They too had suffered tragedy and disappointment, which they could freely talk about, but their humor and genuine interest in life made us feel like their comrades. To us they were models.

AN EXCITING JOURNEY

The maturing marriage lived with thankfulness contains celebrations for the gifts which have been received in the great adventure. Seeing a newlywed couple one can only marvel as an older couple did of us, "Just think how far they have to go and how much they have to learn!" When we overheard this remark we felt small—as if they were the veterans peering down at us as though we were the rookies, which we were. Yet as we evaluate things at this time in our life we realize we *did* have things to learn. But we are glad we embarked on the journey. It has been a pleasure!

Although to arrive we have to take a journey, in the journey of marriage we never really arrive. Rather we are engaged in a process of arriving. There are failures and imperfections on this journey. These go with life, including married life, in a fallen world.

We cannot have it all, though in our insatiable desire for perfection and completion, we desire it all. Commercial advertising takes advantage of this desire. By acquiring this or that product we are assured we are on the way to having it all. How much of our national economy is based on exploiting this weakness?

Lured by seductive advertising and encouraged by other influences in our culture, we seek to have it all. So failures and imperfections, disappointments and reversals, losses and rejections are hard to deal with. We do not want to lose out on anything because "loser" is one of our culture's most derogatory epithets. Other couples seem to have more: he has a more attractive wife or she has a more high-powered husband, or their children seem more advanced than ours, or they have grandchildren and we do not, or their children and grandchildren live in the community while ours live far away, and on and on go the unfavorable comparisons.

Marriages have their ups and downs, just as persons do, but God is bigger than either. God can use both the ups and downs for our marital growth. We have the power to do things differently rather than to remain imprisoned in previously unprofitable ways—even though they are accustomed ways. Anything that seems to fix our relationship at a superficial level will stymie our growth and needs to be challenged. Taking risks by suggesting changes or informing the other of our needs places us in a vulnerable position. Yet we need to do this. By the same token we need to dare to listen to our partner's needs and suggestions, for it probably takes as much courage to listen as to inform. It is so easy to feel accused by such sharing and to become defensive. But when we are big enough to trust in the bigness of God, we can use these times as breakthroughs to deeper levels of relating. You and your partner together can set goals for meeting your needs and plan the steps that you can take *now* toward moving in the direction of these goals. This is a much better way than letting things go on which bother you simply because it is hard to make a decision to act and to carry through on it.

Because each such risk leaves us vulnerable, we could be disappointed by our partner's response or even hurt. Even if such is not the case the venture itself can take us into unfamiliar behaviors in our marriage, and this can be scary. This is the nature of risk and needs to be faced beforehand, so that the possible consequences of the risk can be considered prior to making the decision to take it. Yet even though some possible consequences are not what we would desire, we need to remind ourselves that we are undergirded by our prior marriage with Christ. This is the "inner dialogue" that provides the balance when disappointments threaten to unbalance us. Our covenant with Christ holds firm. Saint Paul rose to heights of eloquence in describing the firmness of this bond. "For I am sure that neither death, nor life, nor angels, nor principalities, nor things present, nor things to come, nor powers, nor height, nor depth, nor anything else in all creation, will be able to separate us from the love of God in Christ Jesus our Lord" (Rom. 8:38). So consider seriously taking the risks to improve your marital relationship so that more of its potential can be actualized. The more initiative you take, the more possibilities you will explore, and your marriage will continue to grow through the years. It is an exciting journey.

The basis of our survival as marital partners is the grace of God—always present, always abounding. With this grace comes the hope of our calling—that God is at work on our behalf, willing the growth of our marriage. We are not "twisting his arm" when we ask for his guidance and help; rather God is "twisting our arm" to ask. God wants to work with us and through us. What may keep us going during darker days is the belief that God is *for* our marriage. Therefore even setbacks in our relationship are within God's redemptive providence.

Setbacks are hard to take. When I asked a former student how he was faring, he said, "Not very well. When my wife and I were not getting along we entered into counseling and made considerable progress. But as time went on we slipped back into our old ways. Now it seems worse than before—because we thought things were better." When marriages regress—and even good ones can do so—it seems to the partners that they are right back where they started. But really they are not. The setback has new insights for them if they are open to receive. But the disillusion and discouragement that accompany setbacks can block this openness.

How, then, can we deal with regressions? The answer is, through forgiveness. As irrational as it may seem there is no limit on how frequently forgiveness can be given. Peter probably had a specific brother in mind when he asked Jesus, " 'Lord, how often shall my brother sin against me, and I forgive him? As many as seven times?' Jesus said to him, 'I do not say to you seven times, but seventy times seven' " (Matt. 18:22).

There is no way forward after a setback without forgiveness. Forgiveness is no substitute for changed behavior, but it is always the first step toward changed behavior. The frank facing of our failure to act constructively and the willingness to seek counseling to effect change in our behavior may need to follow forgiveness. But forgiveness is the beginning and the end for all change. God the giver of forgiveness ever gives, so also we the receivers can give—to our mate, to our self, to our marriage—and in so giving, also receive again. As our divine spouse, God not only forgives without counting the times, he also even *forgets*. "I, am he who blots out your transgressions for my own sake, and I will not remember your sins" (Isa. 43:25).

Notes

CHAPTER 1

1. Gerhard Frost, lecture, Roseville Lutheran Church, St. Paul, Minn., May 18, 1979.
2. Lesley Darmen, "Bring Back the Bad Girls," *McCalls* (April 1985): 162.
3. Edward Dolnic, "Opposites Attract, but Kissing Cousins Hold Fast," *The St. Paul Pioneer Press* (May 10, 1985): 1D.
4. Hugh Misseldine, *Your Inner Child of the Past* (New York: Simon & Schuster, 1963), 68-69.

CHAPTER 2

1. Henri Nouwen, *Reaching Out* (Garden City, N.Y.: Doubleday & Co., 1975), 28.
2. Dan Kiley, *The Peter Pan Syndrome* (New York: Dodd, Mead & Co., 1983), 16, 115.
3. M. Scott Peck, *The Road Less Travelled* (New York: Simon & Schuster, 1978), 155.
4. *A Portrait of the Women of the American Lutheran Church* (Minneapolis: Search Institute, 1980).
5. George R. Bach, workshop held at the University of California at San Diego, April 1976.
6. George R. Bach and Peter Wyden, *The Intimate Enemy* (New York: Avon Books, 1968), 368, 369.
7. Paul Tillich, "To Whom Much Is Forgiven," in *The New Being* (New York: Charles Scribner's Sons, 1955), 13.
8. Ibid., 7.
9. Katherine Anne Porter, "The Necessary Enemy," in *Elements of the Essay*, ed. H. Wendell Smith (Belmont, Calif.: Wadsworth Publishing, 1979), 240.
10. Ibid.

11. George R. Bach, *Creative Aggression* (New York: Avon Books, 1974), 209.

CHAPTER 3

1. Liz Harris, "A Reporter at Large—Holy Days I," *New Yorker* (Sept. 16, 1985): 92.
2. Judy Syfers, "I Want a Wife," *MS. Magazine* (December 1971); reprinted in *Elements of the Essay*, ed. Smith, 72.
3. Student essay, Minneapolis Community College, winter 1982.
4. A. Don Augsburger, ed., *Marriages That Work* (Scottdale, Pa.: Herald Press, 1984), 1.
5. Review by Carla Waldeman of Linda T. Sanford and Mary E. Donovan, *Women and Self-Esteem* (Baltimore: Penguin Books, 1985), in *Skyway News* (Oct. 16-27, 1985): 26.
6. Ellen Goodman, "The Family/Career Priority," in *Patterns*, ed. Mary Lou Conlin (Boston: Houghton Mifflin, 1983), 112.
7. Augsburger, *Marriages That Work*, 14.
8. Kiley, *Peter Pan Syndrome*, 218.
9. Frost, lecture, Roseville Lutheran Church.
10. Wayne Dyer, "How to Make Your Kids Feel Good about Themselves," *Family Circle* (July 10, 1984): 14.
11. G. Douglas Lewis, *Resolving Church Conflicts* (San Francisco: Harper & Row, 1981), 37.
12. Mel Krantzler, *Creative Marriage* (New York: McGraw-Hill, 1981), xii, xiii, 4.
13. Soren Kierkegaard, *Sickness unto Death* (Princeton: Princeton University Press, 1980), 86.
14. "Career Oriented Women Suffer Macho Stress," *USA Today* (April 19, 1985): 4D.

CHAPTER 4

1. William Sloane Coffin, *The Courage to Love* (San Francisco: Harper & Row, 1983), 64.
2. Ibid.
3. Helen Paulsen MacInnes, "When a Child Dies," *The Christian Ministry* (January 1979): 32-33.
4. Carson McCullers, "A Tree. A Rock. A Cloud," in *The Loners*, ed. L. M. Schulman (New York: Macmillan Co., 1970), 274.
5. Vera Mace, lecture, Macalester College, St. Paul, Minn., April 1980.
6. Nouwen, *Reaching Out*, 43.

CHAPTER 5

1. William Hulme et al., *Pastors in Ministry* (Minneapolis: Augsburg Publishing House, 1985).

Notes

2. Paul Tournier, *The Meaning of Persons* (New York: Harper & Brothers, 1957).

CHAPTER 6

1. Malcolm Cowley, *The View from Eighty* (New York: Viking Press, 1980), 5.
2. Kierkegaard, *Sickness unto Death*, 59.
3. Fritz Kunkel, *In Search of Maturity* (New York: Charles Scribner's Sons, 1951), 287.
4. Betty Bumpers, "Mrs. America for Peace," *Parade* (March 2, 1986): 12-14.
5. T. S. Eliot, *Four Quartets, Little Gidding* (New York: Harcourt, Brace & Co., 1943), portion 5.